THE 4 CHORD UKULELE SONGBOOK

*The Beatles • Johnny Cash • Donovan • Simon & Garfunkel
Hank Williams • John Denver • Harry Belafonte
Dave Matthews Band • Little Feat • Buffalo Springfield
Kenny Rogers • The Marshall Tucker Band • Jack Johnson
Elvis Presley • Van Morrison • The Black Eyed Peas
Bruno Mars • Colbie Caillat • Dion • The Beach Boys*

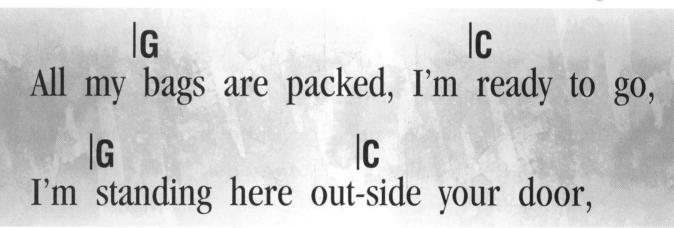

*Peter, Paul, and Mary • The Byrds • Bob Dylan • Crosby, Stills & Nash
Tony Orlando and Dawn • The Youngbloods • Hanson • The Who
Creedence Clearwater Revival • Janis Joplin • Woody Guthrie
Tom Paxton • Bobbie Gentry • Bobby Darin • Bob Marley*

Cherry Lane Music Company
Director of Publications/Project Editor: Mark Phillips

ISBN 978-1-4803-0835-0

Visit our website at www.cherrylaneprint.com

CONTENTS

Act Naturally

Words and Music by
Vonie Morrison and Johnny Russell

D   G   A7   E7

1 2 3   1 3 2   1   1 2 3

Verse 1

| **D** | | | **G** | | |
They're gonna put me in the movies;

| **D** | | | **A7** | |
They're gonna make a big star out of me.

| **D** | | | **G** | |
We'll make a scene about a man that's sad and lonely,

| **A7** | | | **D** | |
And all I gotta do is   act natural - ly.

Verse 2

‖ **D** | | | **G** | |
We'll make a score about a man that's sad and lonely

| **D** | | | **A7** | |
And beggin' down up - on his bended knee.

| **D** | | | **G** | |
I'll play the part but I won't need re - hearsin',

| **A7** | | | **D** | |
'Cause all I have to do is   act natural - ly.

Bridge

|| A7 | | D |

Well, I bet you I'm gonna be a big star.

| A7 | | D |

Might win an Ocsar; you can't never tell.

| A7 | | D |

The movies are gonna make me a big star,

| E7 | | A7 |

'Cause I can play the part so well.

Verse 3

|| D | | G | |

Well, I hope you come and see me in the movies,

D | | A7 |

Then I know that you will plainly see

| D | | G |

The biggest fool that ever hit the big time,

| A7 | | D | ||

And all I gotta do is   act natural - ly.

All Shook Up

Words and Music by
Otis Blackwell and Elvis Presley

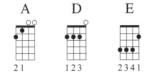

Intro

A | | |

Verse 1

            ‖A |
A-well-a, bless my soul, what's wrong with me?
     |A |
I'm itching like a man on a fuzzy tree.
      |A |
My friends say I'm acting wild as a bug.
       |A N.C. |
I'm in love!   I'm all shook up!
      |D |E |A |
Ooh, ooh, yeah, yeah, yeah.

Verse 2

            ‖A |
Well, my hands are shaky and my knees are weak;
   |A | |
I can't seem to stand on my own two feet.
A |
Who do you thank when you have such luck?
      |A N.C. |
I'm in love!   I'm all shook up!
      |D |E |A |
Ooh, ooh, yeah, yeah, yeah.

Bridge 1

‖**D** |

Well, please don't ask me what's on my mind;

|**A** |

I'm a little mixed up but I feel fine.

|**D** |

When I'm near that girl that I love best,

|**E**   **N.C.** |

My heart beats so it scares me to death!

Verse 3

‖**A** |

When she touched   my hand what a chill I got;

|**A** | |

Her lips are like a vol - cano that's hot!

A |

I'm proud to say that she's my buttercup.

|**A** **N.C.** |

I'm in love!   I'm all shook up!

|**D** |**E** |**A** |

Ooh, ooh, yeah, yeah, yeah.

Bridge 2

‖**D** |

My tongue gets tied when I try to speak;

|**A** |

My insides shake like a leaf on a tree.

|**D** |

There's only one cure for this body of mine:

|**E**   **N.C.** |

That's to have that girl that I love so fine!

Verse 4

‖**A** |
She touched my hand and what a chill I got;

|**A** | |
Her lips are like a vol - cano that's hot!

A |
I'm proud to say that she's my buttercup.

|**A**   **N.C.** |
I'm in love!   I'm all shook up!

|**D** |**E** |**A** |
Ooh, ooh, yeah, yeah, yeah.

|**D** |**E** |**A** | ‖
Ooh, ooh, yeah, yeah. I'm all shook up!

A Boy Named Sue

Words and Music by
Shel Silverstein

G   C   D7

Verse 1

|G |
Well, my "daddy" left home when I was three,

|C |
And he didn't leave much to Ma and me,

|D7 | |G |
Just this old guitar and an empty bottle of booze.

|G |
Now, I don't blame him because he run and hid,

|C | |D7
But the meanest thing that he ever did was be - fore he left,

|D7 |G |
He went and named me Sue.

Verse 2

‖G |
Well, he must have thought it was quite a joke,

|C |
And it got lots of laughs from a lot of folks.

|D7 | |G |
It seems I had to fight my whole life through.

|G |
Some gal would giggle and I'd get red.

|C |
And some guy would laugh and I'd bust his head,

|D7 | |G |
I tell you, life ain't easy for a boy named Sue.

Verse 3

```
        ‖G                    |
Well, I grew up quick and I grew up mean.

     |C                    |                |
My fist got hard and my wits got keen.

D7                     |              |G            |
Roamed from town to town to hide my shame.

     |G                    |                |
But I made me a vow to the moon and stars,

C                  |
I'd search the honky - tonks and bars

     |D7               |                      |G        |
And kill that man that give me that awful name.
```


Verse 4

```
        ‖G              |
But it was Gatlinburg in mid July,

        |C               |                |
And I had just hit town and my throat was dry.

D7                      |              |G            |
  I'd thought I'd stop and have myself a brew.

     |G                    |                |
At an old saloon on a street of mud,

C                |            |
There at a table dealing stud

D7                     |               |G        |
Sat the dirty, mangy dog that named me Sue.
```

Verse 5

|| G |

Well, I knew that snake was my own sweet dad

| C |

From a worn-out picture that my mother had.

| D7 | | G |

And I knew that scar on his cheek and his evil eye.

| G |

He was big and bent and gray and old

| C |

And I looked at him and my blood ran cold,

| D7 | G |

And I said "My name is Sue.   How do you do?

| G | | | | |

Now you're gonna die."   Yeah that's what I told him.

Verse 6

|| G | |

Well, I hit him hard right be - tween the eyes and

C

    He went down, But to my surprise

D7 | | G |

    He come up with a knife and cut off a piece of my ear.

| G |

But I busted a chair right a - cross his teeth,

| C |

And we crashed through the wall and into the street,

D7 | | G |

Kicking and a-gouging in the mud and the blood and the beer.

Verse 7

```
 ‖G                    |              |
I tell you I've fought tougher men but I

C                       |
Really can't remember when.

  |D7                   |          |G           |
He kicked like a mule and he bit like a croco - dile.

  |G                    |
I heard him laugh and then I heard him cuss,

     |C                 |
And he went for his gun and I pulled mine first.

  |D7                   |            |G         |
He stood there looking at me      and I saw him smile.
```

Verse 8

```
         ‖G       |       |              |
And he said, "Son,     this world is rough and if a man's gonna make it,

  |G              |              |D7              |G      |
He's gotta be tough, and I know I wouldn't be there to help you a - long.

     |G           |
So I give you that name and I said goodbye,

  |C              |
I knew you'd have to get tough   or die.

     |D7          |              |G        |
And it's that name that helped to make you strong."
```

Verse 9

```
      ‖G          |              |
Yeah,    he said, "Now, you just fought one helluva fight,

     |C           |
And I know you hate me and you've got the right

  |D7             |              |G        |
To kill me now and I wouldn't blame you if you do.

     |G           |
But you ought to thank me be - fore I die

     |C           |
For the gravel in your guts and the spit in your eye

     |D7          |       |G        |
'Cause I'm the ——      that named you Sue."

     |G           |            |C
Yeah, what could I do?   What could I do?
```

Verse 10

        ‖C   **|D7**
I got all choked up and I threw down my gun

      |D7   **|G**
And called him my pa and he called me his son,

G   **|**   **|**   **|D7**
And I come away with a different point of view.

      |G   **|**
And I think about him now and then.

      |C   **|**   **|D7 N.C.**
Every time I tried, every time I win,   and if I ever have a son

N.C.   **|G**   **‖**
I think I'm gonna name him ... Bill or George! ... anything but Sue!

Brown Eyed Girl

Words and Music by
Van Morrison

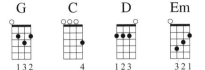

Intro   G |C |G |D |G |C |G |D ||

Verse 1

G |C |
Hey, where did we   go?
G |D |
Days when the rains   came,
G |C |
Down in the hol - low,
G |D |
Playing a new   game.
G |C |
Laughing and a-running, hey, hey,
G |D |
Skipping and a-jumping.
G |C |
In the misty morn - ing fog
      |G |D |C |
With   our, hearts a-thumping, and you,
D |G |Em |
My brown-eyed girl.
C |D |G |D ||
You, my   brown-eyed girl.

Verse 2

```
      G              |C              |
And whatever hap - pened
      G                    |D              |
   To Tuesday and so    slow?
      G                    |C              |
   Going down the old   mine with a
      G          |D              |
   Transistor ra - dio.
      G                    |C              |
   Standing in the sunlight laughing,
      G              |D              |
   Hiding 'hind a rainbow's wall.
      G                    |C              |
   Slipping and a-slid - ing
      G              |D              |C              |
   All along the waterfall with you,
   D                    |G          |Em              |
   My brown-eyed girl.
   C          |D          |G              |
   You, my    brown-eyed girl.
   D7              |              |              ||
   Do you remem - ber when    we used to sing:
```

Chorus

```
      G              |C          |G              |D              |
   Sha, la, la, la,  la, la, la, la,  la, la, la, te, da.   Just like that.
      G              |C          |G              |D
   Sha, la, la, la,  la, la, la, la,  la, la, la, te, da,
                  |G          |          ||
La, te, da.
```

Interlude   G | | |C |G |D ||

Verse 3

G |C |
So hard to find my way

G |D |
Now that I'm all on my own.

G |C |
I saw you just the other day;

G |D |
My, how you have grown.

G |C |
Cast my memory back there, Lord.

G |D |
Sometimes I'm over - come thinking about it.

G |C |
Makin' love in the green grass

G |D |C |
Behind the stadium with you,

D |G |Em |
My brown-eyed girl.

C |D |G |
You, my brown-eyed girl.

D | | ||
Do you remem - ber when we used to sing:

Outro

G |C |G |D |
Sha, la, la, la, la, la, la, la, la, la, la, te, da.

G |C |G |D |G ||
Sha, la, la, la, la, la, la, la, la, la, la, te, da.

Digging a Ditch

Lyrics by David J. Matthews
Music by Dave Matthews Band

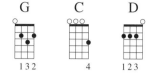

Verse 1

    G |**C** |
Run to your dreaming when   you're alone.
    G |**C** |
Unplug the TV and turn off your phone.
    G |**C**
Get heavy on with digging your ditch.

Chorus 1

        ‖**G** |**C** |
'Cause I'm   digging a ditch where madness   gives a bit.
    G |**C** |
Digging a ditch where silence   lives.
    G |**C** |
Digging a ditch for when I'm   old.
    G |**C**
Digging this ditch, my story's   told.
        |**G** |**C**   ‖
Where all   these troubles that weigh down on me will rise.

Verse 2

  G   **|C**
  Run to your dreaming when you're alone.
      |G   **|C**
Where all these questions spinning a - round my head
      |D   **|C**
Will die,
      |D   **|C**   **||**
Will die,   will die.

Repeat Verse 1

Chorus 2

      ||G   **|C**   **|**
'Cause I'm digging a ditch where madness gives a bit.
G   **|C**   **|**
 Digging a ditch where silence lives.
G   **|C**   **|**
 Digging a ditch for when I'm through.
G   **|C**
 Digging this ditch, I'm digging for you.
    |G   **|C**
Where all these worries that wear down on me
    |G   **|C**
Will rise.
    |G   **|C**   **||**
Where all these habits that pull heavy at my heart will die.

Verse 3

```
     G                              |C                    |
  Run  to  your  dreaming  when  you're  alone.
     G                                |C
  Not  what  you  should  be  or  what    you've  become.
       |G                |C
Just   get  heavy  on  with  digging  your  ditch.
```

Chorus 3

```
                    ‖G                          |C              |
'Cause  I'm    digging  a  ditch  where  madness    gives  a  bit.
     G                            |C            |
   Digging  a  ditch  where  silence    lives.
       |G                          |C
Where  all    these  disappointments  that  grow  angry  out  of  me
         |D              |C
Will  rise,
         |D                |C
Will  die,
         |D                  |C              ‖
Will  die,                        will  die.
```

Repeat Verse 1

Catch the Wind

Words and Music by Donovan Leitch

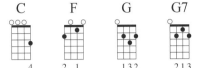

Verse 1

|C | |F | |
In the chilly hours and minutes,

|C | |F | | |
Of un - certainty,   I want to be

C | |F |G |C | |G7 |
In the warm   hold of your loving mind.

|C | |F | |
To feel you all a - round me,

|C | |F | | |
And to take your hand a - long the sand,

C | |F |G |C | |G7 |
Ah, but I may as well try and catch the wind.

Verse 2

|| **C** | | **F** | |
When sundown pales the sky,

| **C** | | **F** | | |
I want to hide a - while, behind your smile.

C | | **F** | **G** | **C** | | **G7** |
And everywhere I'd look, your eyes I'd find.

| **C** | | **F** | |
For me to love you now,

| **C** | **F** | | |
Would be the sweetest thing, 'twould make me sing,

C | | **F** | **G** | **C** | | **G7** |
Ah, but I may as well try and catch the wind.

Verse 3

|| **C** | | **F** | | |
When rain has hung the leaves with tears,

C | | **F** | | |
I want you near to kill my fears,

C | | **F** | **G** | **C** | | **G7** |
To help me to leave all my blues be - hind.

| **C** | | **F** | |
For standing in your heart

| **C** | | **F** | | |
Is where I want to be, and long to be,

C | | **F** | **G** | **C** | | ||
Ah, but I may as well try and catch the wind.

Cecilia

Words and Music by Paul Simon

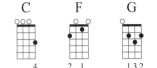

Chorus 1

C |F   C
Celia, you're breaking my heart.

    |F   C |G
You're shaking my con - fidence dai - ly.

    |F C |F   C
Oh Ce - cil - ia, I'm down on my knees.

    |F   C |G
I'm begging you please to come home.

Chorus 2

C |F   C
Celia, you're breaking my heart.

    |F   C |G
You're shaking my con - fidence dai - ly.

    |F C |F   C
Oh Ce - cil - ia, I'm down on my knees.

    |F   C |G |C
I'm begging you please to come home, come on home.

Verse

C |F |C
Making love in the af - ternoon with Cecil - ia

F |G   C |
Up in my bedroom (making love).

C |F
I got up to wash my face.

    |C |G   C ||
When I come back to bed someone's tak - en my place.

Chorus 3

C |F   C
Celia, you're breaking my heart.

   |F   C |G
You're shaking my con - fidence dai - ly.

    |F C |F   C
Oh Ce - cil - ia, I'm down on my knees.

   |F   C |G |C
I'm begging you please to come home, come on home.

Interlude

    ||F | |G
Poh poh poh poh poh poh poh poh poh poh poh poh poh.

Bridge

    ||F C |F   C
Jubi - la - tion, she loves me again.

  |F   C |G
I fall on the floor and I'm laugh - ing.

   |F C |F   C
Jubi - la - tion, she loves me again.

  |F   C |G
I fall on the floor and I'm laugh - ing.

Tag

    ||F C |F   C
Oh oh oh oh oh oh oh oh oh

  |F   C |G |C ||
Oh oh oh oh oh oh oh oh oh, come on home.

Cold, Cold Heart

Words and Music by
Hank Williams

E   B7   E7   A

Verse 1

|E | | |B7
I tried so hard, my dear, to show that you're my every dream.

|B7 | | |E
Yet you're afraid each thing I do is just some evil scheme.

|E | |E7 |A
A memory from your lonesome past keeps us so far a - part.

|B7 | | |E
Why can't I free your doubtful mind and melt your cold, cold heart?

Verse 2

||E | | |B7
An - other love be - fore my time made your heart sad and blue.

|B7 | | |E
And so my heart is paying now for things I didn't do.

|E | |E7 |A
In anger unkind words are said that make the teardrops start.

|B7 | | |E
Why can't I free your doubtful mind and melt your cold, cold heart?

Verse 3

    ‖**E** | | |**B7**
You'll never know how much it hurts to see you sit and cry.

    |**B7** | | |**E**
You know you need and want my love, yet you're afraid to try.

    |**E** | |**E7** |**A**
Why do you run and hide from life? To try it just ain't smart.

    |**B7** | | |**E**
Why can't I free your doubtful mind and melt your cold, cold heart?

Verse 4

    ‖**E** | | |**B7**
There was a time when I believed that you belonged to me.

    |**B7** | | |**E**
But now I know your heart is shackled to a memo - ry.

    |**E** | |**E7** |**A**
The more I learn to care for you the more we drift a - part.

    |**B7** | | |**E**   ‖
Why can't I free your doubtful mind and melt your cold, cold heart.

Dancing with the Mountains

Words and Music by
John Denver

D   G   Em   A

123   132   321   21

Verse 1

D
Everybody's got the dancin' fever,

D
Everybody loves to rock and roll.

D
Play it louder, baby, play it faster,

D
Funky music's gotta stretch your soul.

Verse 2

D
Just relax and let the rhythm take you,

D
Don't you be afraid to lose control.

D
If your heart has found some empty spaces,

D
Dancin's just a thing to make you whole.

Chorus 1

```
G                        |              |D        |        |
I am one who dances with the moun-tains.

G                    |          |D      |      |
I am one who dances in the wind.

G                |          |D        |
I am one who dances on the o-cean.

    |G                |Em       A        |D        |        ||
My partner's more than pieces,     more than friends.
```

Verse 3

```
D                          |                    |
Were you there the night they lost the lightning?

D                        |                |
Were you there the day the earth stood still?

D                      |                |
Did you see the famous and the fighting?

D                      |            ||
Did you hear the prophet tell his tale?
```

Chorus 2

```
G                    |                |D      |        |
We are one when dancing with the moun-tains.

G                |                |D      |      |
We are one when singing in the wind.

G              |            |D      |
We are one when thinking of each oth-er,

    |G              |Em       A      |D        |          ||
More than partners, more than pieces,     more than friends.
```

Day-O
(The Banana Boat Song)

Words and Music by
Irving Burgie and William Attaway

D   A7

Intro

N.C.(D)
Day-o, day-o.

Daylight come and me wan' go home.

Day, me say day, me say day, me say day, me say day, me say day-o.

Daylight come and me wan' go home.

Verse 1

D
Work all night on a drink of rum.

D   A7   D
Daylight come and me wan' go home.

D
Stack banana till de morning come.

D   A7   D
Daylight come and me wan' go home.

Verse 2

D   A7
Come, mister tally man, tally me banana.

D   A7   D
Daylight come and me wan' go home.

D   A7
Come, mister tally man, tally me banana.

D   A7   D
Daylight come and me wan' go home.

Verse 3

‖**D**
Lift six-hand, seven-hand, eight-hand bunch.

D | **A7** **D** |
Daylight come and me wan' go home.

D |
Six-hand, seven-hand, eight-hand bunch.

D | **A7** **D** ‖
Daylight come and me wan' go home.

Chorus

D |
Day, me say day-o.

D | **A7** **D** |
Daylight come and me wan' go home.

D |
Day, me say day, me say day, me say…

D | **A7** **D**
Daylight come and me wan' go home.

Verse 4

‖**D** |
A beautiful bunch of ripe banana.

D | **A7** **D** |
Daylight come and me wan' go home.

D |
Hide the deadly black tarantula.

D | **A7** **D** ‖
Daylight come and me wan' go home.

Repeat Chorus

Repeat Verse 2

Outro

N.C.(D) | |
Day-o, day-o.

D | **A7** **D** |
Daylight come and me wan' go home.

N.C.(D) | | |
Day, me say day, me say day, me say day, me say day, me say day-o.

D | **A7** **D** ‖
Daylight come and me wan' go home.

Dixie Chicken

Words and Music by Lowell George
and Martin Kibbee

A   E   D

Verse 1

|A |
I've seen the bright lights of Mem - phis

|A |E7
And the Commodore Hotel,

|E7 |
And underneath a street   lamp

|E7 |A
I met   a Southern belle.

|D |A |
Oh, she took me to the riv - er,

A |E7
Where she cast her spell,

|E7 |
And in the Southern moon - light

|E7 |A
She sang   her song so well.

Chorus

    ‖**A** |

If you be my Dixie chick - en

    |**A** |**E7**

I'll be your Tennessee lamb,

    |**E7** |

And we can walk togeth - er

       |**A** | | |

Down in Dixieland,   down in Dix - ieland.

Verse 2

    ‖**A** |

Well,   we made all the hot   spots;

    |**A** |**E7**

My   money flowed like wine.

    |**E7** |

And that low-down Southern whis - key

    |**E7** |**A**

Began   to fog my mind.

    |**D** |**A**

And I don't remember church   bells

    |**A** |**E7**

Or the money I put down

    |**E7** |

On the white picket fence and board - walk

    |**E7** |**A**

Of the house at the edge of town.

    |**D** |**A**

Oh, but boy, do I remem - ber

    |**A** |**E7**

The strain of her refrain

    |**E7** |

And the nights   we spent togeth - er

    |**E7** |**A**

And the way she called my name.

Repeat Chorus

Verse 3

     ‖**A** |
Well,   been a year since she   ran away;

           |**A** |**E7**
Guess that guitar player sure could play.

     |**E7** |
She always liked to sing   along;

        |**E7** |**A** |
She's al - ways handy with   a song.

D |**A**
Then one night in the lobby

      |**A** |**E7**
Of the Commodore Hotel,

  |**E7** |
I chanced to meet a bartend - er

  |**E7** |**A**
Who said he knew her well.

   |**D** |**A**
And as he handed me   a drink,

   |**A** |**E7**
He be - gan to hum a song,

   |**E7** |
And all   the boys there at   the bar

  |**E7** |**A**
Be - gan to sing along.

Repeat Chorus

Don't Be Cruel
(To a Heart That's True)

Words and Music by
Otis Blackwell and Elvis Presley

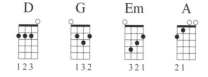

Intro | D | | |

Verse 1
|| D | |
You know I can be found
D |
Sitting home all alone.
| G |
If you can't come around,
| D |
At least please telephone.
| Em |
Don't be cruel
A | D | ||
To a heart that's true.

Verse 2

D
Baby, if I made you mad
  |D | |
For something I might have said,
G
Please, let's forget my past;
  |D
The future looks bright ahead.
      |Em
Don't be cruel
A |D
    To a heart that's true.

Bridge 1

      ||G |A
I don't want no other love.
G |A |D
Baby, it's still you I'm thinking of.

Verse 3

    ||D
Don't stop thinking of me,
   |D
Don't make me feel this way,
  |G
Come on over here and love me.
   |D
You know what I want you to say.
     |Em
Don't be cruel
A |D
    To a heart that's true.

Bridge 2

```
    ‖G                    |A
Why should we be apart?
    |G              |A            |D          |
I really love you, ba - by, cross my heart.
```

Verse 4

```
    ‖D                    |
Let's walk up to the preach - er
    |D          |        |
And let us say, "I do."
G                        |
Then you'll know you'll have me
    |D              |
And I'll know that I'll have you.
    |Em          |
Don't be cruel
A                |D          |
To a heart that's true.
```

Repeat Bridge 1

Outro

```
        ‖Em          |
Don't be cruel
A                  |D        |
To a heart that's true.
        |Em          |
Don't be cruel
A                  |D        |
To a heart that's true.
    |G                  |A        |
I don't want no other love.
G              |A          |D        |        ‖
Baby, it's still you  I'm thinking of.
```

For What It's Worth

Words and Music by
Stephen Stills

E   A   D

2 3 4 1   2 1   1 2 3

Verse 1

E |A
There's something happening here.
|E |A
What it is ain't exactly clear.
|E |A
There's a man with a gun over there
|E |A
Telling me I got to beware.
|E D |
I think it's time we stop, children. What's that sound?
A |
Everybody look what's goin' down.
E |A |E |A ||

Verse 2

E |A
There's battle lines being drawn.
|E |A |
Nobody's right if everybody's wrong.
E |A
Young people speakin' their minds,
|E |A
Getting so much resistance from behind.
|E D |
I think it's time we stop, hey. What's that sound?
A |
Everybody look what's goin' down.
E |A |E |A ||

Verse 3

```
        E                        |A
        What a field day for the heat.
    |E                   |A
A thousand people in the street
        |E                      |A
Singin' songs and carryin' signs,
        |E                       |A
Mostly say, "Hooray for our side."
              |E        D              |
It's time we stop, hey. What's that sound?
A                               |
Everybody look what's goin' down.
E               |A          E            |A            ||
```

Verse 4

```
        E          |A                |
Paranoia strikes deep,
E                  |A
Into your life it will creep.
    |E                      |A
It starts when you're always afraid.
              |E
Step out of line, the man come
    |A
And take you away.
```

Outro

        ‖E   D |
We better stop, hey. What's that sound?

A
Everybody look what's goin'...

        |E   D |
You better stop, hey. What's that sound?

A
Everybody look what's goin'...

        |E   D |
You better stop, now. What's that sound?

A
Everybody look what's goin'...

        |E   D |
You better stop, children. What's that sound?

A |E   D |A |E   ‖
Everybody look what's goin'...

The Horizon Has Been Defeated

Words and Music by Jack Johnson

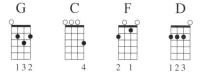

Verse 1

      |G   C
(The) ho - rizon has been defeat - ed

    |F   G |
By the pirates of the new age.

G   C
Alien casi - nos,

  |F   G
Well, maybe it's just time to say

 |G   C
That things can go bad

 |F   G
And make you want to run away.

 |G |C
But as we grow old - er,

 |F |D | ||
The trouble just seems to stay.

Verse 2

    G   **C**
Future complica - tions

       |F   **G**
In the strings between the cans.

      |G   **C**
But no prints can come from fin - gers

       |F   **G**
If ma - chines become our hands.

          |G   **C**
And then our feet become the wheels,

         |F   **G**
And then the wheels become the cars.

         |G   **C**
And then the rigs begin to drill

       |F   **|D** | ‖
Until the drilling goes too   far.

Chorus

    G   **C**
Things can go bad

     |F   **G**
And make you want to run away.

     |G   **C**
But as we grow old - er,

      |F   **|D**   **C**   **|G**   **|D**   **C**   **|G**   ‖
(The) ho - rizon begins to   fade, fade, fade,   fade away.

Verse 3

```
G                    C            |
Thingamajigsaw  puz - zled;

F                              G        |
Anger,  don't  you  step  too  close.

       |G
'Cause  people  are  lonely

         C       |F                 G        |
And  on - ly  ani - mals  with  fancy  shoes.

G                    C            |
Hallelujah  zig  zag  noth - ing;

F                          G
Misery,  it's  on  the  loose.

       |G
'Cause  people  are  lonely

         C       |F                         |
And  on - ly  ani - mals  with  too  many  tools

D                                          |
   That  can  build  all  the  junk  that  we  sell.

D                                          ||
Oh,  sometime,  man,  make  you  want  to  yell,  and….
```

Chorus

```
G                    C
Things  can  go  bad

     |F                     G
And  make  you  want  to  run  away.

     |G            C
But  as  we  grow  old - er,

         |F           |D   C    |G         |D   C    |G        |
(The)  ho - rizon  begins  to   fade   away,         fade   away.

D      C    |G        |
   Fade,  fade,  fade.

D      C    |G            ||
   Fade,  fade,  fade.
```

The Gambler

Words and Music by
Don Schlitz

D G A

Verse 1

|D |G |D
On a warm summer's eve - nin' on a train bound for no - where,

|D | | |A
I met up with the gam - bler; we were both too tired to sleep.

|D | |G |D
So we took turns star - in' out the window at the dark - ness

|G |D |A |D
Till boredom overtook us   and he began to speak.

Verse 2

‖D | |G |D
He said, "Son I've made a life   out of readin' people's fac - es

|D | | |A
And knowin' what their cards were   by the way they held their eyes.

|D | |G |D
And if you don't mind my say - in', I can see you're out of ac - es.

|G |D |A |D |
For a taste of your whis - key I'll give you some advice."

Verse 3

‖D | |G |D |
So I handed him my bot - tle and he drank down my last swallow.

D | | |A
Then he bummed a cig - arette and asked me for a light.

|D | |G |D
And the night got deathly qui - et, and his face lost all expres - sion.

|G |D |A |D
Said, "If you're gonna play the game, boy, ya gotta learn to play it right.

Chorus

||**D** | |
You got to know when to hold 'em,

G |**D** |
Know when to fold 'em,

G |**D** | |**A**
Know when to walk away and know when to run.

|**D** | |**G** |**D**
You never count your money when you're sittin' at the ta - ble.

|**D** **G** |**D** |
There'll be time e - nough for count - in'

A |**D** | ||
When the dealin's done.

Verse 4

D | |**G** |**D**
Ev'ry gambler knows that the secret to surviv - in'

|**D** | | |**A**
Is knowing what to throw away and knowin' what to keep,

|**D** | |**G** |**D**
'Cause ev'ry hand's a win - ner and ev'ry hand's a los - er,

|**G** |**D** |**A** |**D**
And the best that you can hope for is to die in your sleep."

Verse 5

||**D** | |**G** |**D** |
And when he'd finished speakin', he turned back towards the win - dow,

D | | |**A**
Crushed out his cigarette and faded off to sleep.

|**D** | |**G** |**D**
And somewhere in the dark - ness the gambler, he broke even.

|**G** |**D** |**A** |**D**
But in his final words I found an ace that I could keep.

Repeat Chorus

Garden Song

Words and Music by
Dave Mallett

D   G   A

Verse 1

D |G   D |G   A |D |
Inch by inch, row by row,   gonna make this garden grow,

G   A |D |G |A |
All it takes is a rake and a hoe and a piece of fertile ground.

D |G   D |G   A |D |
Inch by inch, row by row,   someone bless the seeds I sow,

G   A |D |G   A |D |G D | |A D ||
Someone warm them from below 'til the rain comes tumbling down.

Verse 2

D |G   D |G   A |D |
Pulling weeds and pickin' stones, man is made of dreams and bones,

G   A |D |G |A |
Feel the need to grow my own 'cause the time is close at hand.

D |G   D |G   A |D |
Grain for grain, sun and rain, find my way in nature's chain,

G   A |D |G   A |D |A |D ||
To my body and my brain to the music from the land.

Verse 3

```
     D              |G              D |G        A      |D              |
     Plant your rows straight and long,  thicker than  with prayer and song,

   G       A      |D                      |G                |A     |
   Mother Earth will make you strong if you give her love and care.

     D              |G      D |G           A    |D        |
     Old crow watchin' hungrily  from his perch  in yonder tree,

   G      A    |D                    |G        A      |D  |A     |D  |A     ||
   In my garden I'm as free as that feathered beak up there.
```

Verse 4

```
     D              |G       D |G    A        |D              |
     Inch by inch, row by row,    gonna make this garden grow,

   G    A      |D                          |G                  |A     |
   All it takes is a rake and a hoe and a piece of fertile ground.

     D         |G          D |G      A        |D              |
     Inch by inch, row by row,    someone bless the seeds I sow,

   G          A    |D                    |G       A      |D    |    |A D ||
   Someone warm   them from below 'til the rain comes tumbling down.
```

Guantanamera
Cuban Folksong

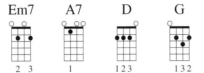

Chorus

Em7   **|A7**   **|**
Guantanamera!   Guajira!

D   **G**   **|A7**   **|**
Guantana - mera!

D   **G**   **|A7**   **|**
Guantana - me - ra!   Guajira!

D   **G**   **|A7**
Guantana - me - ra!

Verse 1

||G   **|A7**
Yo soy un hombre sincero

|D   **G**   **|A7**
De donde crece la palma.

|G   **|A7**
Yo soy un hombre sincero

|G   **|A7**
De donde crece la palma.

|D   **G**   **|A7**
Y antes de morirme quie - ro

|D   **G** **|A7**   **||**
Echar mis versos del al - ma.

Repeat Chorus

Verse 2

                         ‖**G** |**A7**

Mi verso es de un verde claro

                 |**D**   **G** |**A7**

Y de un car - min encen - dido.

                  |**G** |**A7**

Mi verso es de un verde claro

               |**G** |**A7**

Y de un car - min encen - dido.

            |**D**   **G** |**A7**

Mi verso es un cierro heri - do

              |**D**   **G** |**A7** ‖

Que busca en el monte am - pa - ro.

Repeat Chorus

Verse 3

                 ‖**G** |**A7**

Con los po - bres de la tierra

            |**D**   **G** |**A7**

Quiero yo mi suerte e - char.

           |**G** |**A7**

Con los po - bres de la tierra

          |**G** |**A7**

Quiero yo mi suerte e - char

        |**D**   **G** |**A7**

El arro - yo de la si - er - ra

       |**D**   **G** |**A7** ‖

Me compla - ce mas que el mar.

Repeat Chorus

Heard It in a Love Song

Words and Music by Toy Caldwell

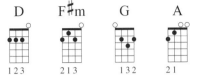

Verse 1

|D | | |
I ain't never been with a woman long enough

F#m | |
For my boots to get old.

G |
We've been togeth - er so long now,

|D | |
They both need re - soled.

D | |
If I ever settle down,

F#m |
You'd be my kind,

|G
And it's a good time for me

|A |D |
To head on down the line.

Chorus

||D A |G | |
Heard it in a love   song.

|D A |G |
Heard it in a love   song.

|D A |G |
Heard it in a love   song.

|D A |G |D ||
Can't be wrong.

Verse 2

D | |
   I'm the kind of man

F♯m | |
    Who likes to get away,

G |
   Likes to start dreaming about

|D | |
To - morrow to - day.

D |
   Never said that I loved you

|F♯m |
Even though it's so.

|G |A
There's that duffle bag of mine;

|D |
It's time to go.

Repeat Chorus

Verse 3

D | |
   I'm gonna be leaving

F♯m | |
    At the break of dawn.

G |
   Wish you could come,

|D | |
But I don't need no woman taggin' a - long.

D |
   Always something greener

|F♯m |
On the other side of that hill.

|G
I was born a wrangler and a rounder

|A |D |
And I guess I always will.

Repeat Chorus

49

The Holly and the Ivy

18th Century English Carol

G   C   D   Em

Verse 1

```
   |G          C  |G
The holly and the ivy

      |G              C  |D
When they are both full grown,

   |G                  |C   G
Of all the trees that are in the wood,

Em |C         D |G    C
The holly bears the crown.
```

Chorus

```
   ||G       C  |G
The rising of the sun

      |G           C  |D
And the running of the deer,

   |G            |C    G  Em
The playing of the merry or-gan,

      |C          D |G
Sweet singing in the choir.
```

Verse 2

```
   ||G        C |G
The holly bears a blossom

   |G        C |D
As white as lil-y flow'r,

   |G              |C    G
And Mary bore sweet Jesus Christ

Em |C         D |G    C
To be our sweet Sav-iour.
```

Repeat Chorus

Verse 3

```
     ‖G            C |G
The  holly bears  a  berry

 |G          C |D
As red  as  an-y  blood,

   |G              |C     G
And  Mary  bore sweet Jesus Christ

Em|C            D  |G    C
To  do  poor  sin-ners  good.
```

Repeat Chorus

Verse 4

```
     ‖G            C|G
The  holly bears  a  prickle

 |G            C |D
As  sharp  as  an-y  thorn,

   |G            |C    G
And  Mary  bore sweet Jesus Christ

Em |C          D  |G    C
On  Christmas Day in  the  morn.
```

Repeat Chorus

I Gotta Feeling

Words and Music by
Will Adams, Allan Pineda, Jaime Gomez, Stacy Ferguson, David Guetta and Frederic Riesterer

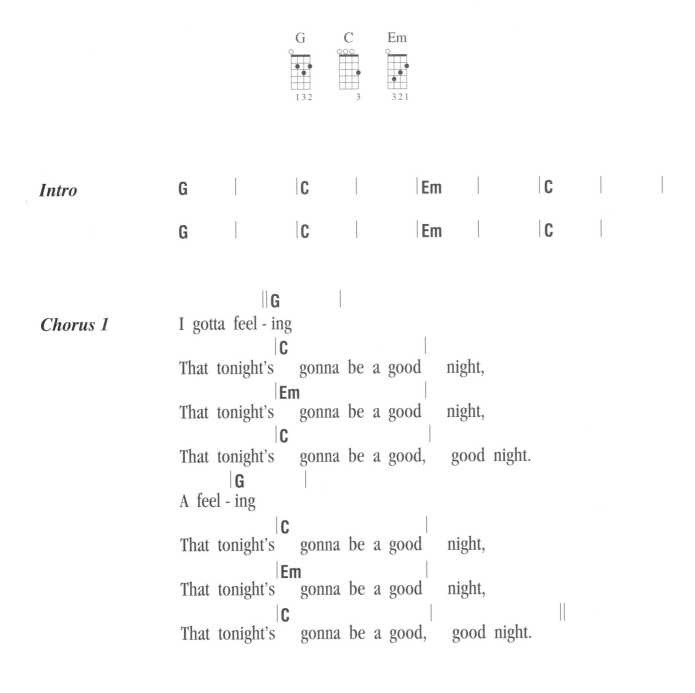

Intro

| G | | C | | Em | | C | | |

| G | | C | | Em | | C | |

Chorus 1

‖ G |

I gotta feel - ing

| C |

That tonight's gonna be a good night,

| Em |

That tonight's gonna be a good night,

| C |

That tonight's gonna be a good, good night.

| G |

A feel - ing

| C |

That tonight's gonna be a good night,

| Em |

That tonight's gonna be a good night,

| C | ‖

That tonight's gonna be a good, good night.

Verse 1

```
G                           |                    |
    Tonight's the night.    Let's live it up.
C                     |                    |
    I got my money.   Let's spend it up.
Em                         |                  |
    Go out and smash it.    Like, oh my God,
C                        |   Tacet          ||
    Jump off that sofa.     Let's get, get  off.
```

Verse 2

```
G                         |
    I know that we'll     have a ball
            |C                            |
If we get   down and go out and just    lose it all.
          |Em                   |
I feel    stressed out. I wan-na let it go.
              |C                       |            ||
Let's go way  out, spaced out and los-ing all control. (Ch-ch-ch-ch.)
```

Verse 3

```
G                    |                  |
    Fill up my cup.      Mazol tov!
C                      |                  |
    Look at her dancing;   just take it   off.
Em                        |                 |
    Let's paint the town.   We'll shut it down.
C                        |                    ||
    Let's burn the roof      and then we'll do it again.
```

Bridge 1

```
     G                                    |C              |
     Let's do it, let's do it, let's do it, let's do it, and do it, and do it.
                          |Em                    |
     Let's live it up, and do it, and do it, and do it, do it, do it.
        |C                        |
     Let's do it. Let's do it.  Let's do it, 'cause
```

Repeat Chorus 1

Repeat Verse 1

Repeat Verse 3

Bridge 2

```
     G                                    |C                 |
     Let's do it, let's do it, let's do it, let's do it, and do it, and do it.
                          |Em                    |
     Let's live it up, and do it, and do it, and do it, do it, do it.
         |C                    |                      ||
     Let's do it. Let's do it.  Let's do it, do it, do it, do it.
```


Verse 4

```
     G                          |                  |
     Here we come, here we go. We gotta rock.
     C                          |              |
     Easy come, easy go. Now we on top.
     Em                          |                  |
     Feel the shot, body rock. Rock it, don't stop.
     C                                |                  ||
     Round and round, up and down, around the clock.
```

Verse 5

```
G                    |                          |
Monday, Tuesday, Wednesday and Thursday.
C                    |                          |
Friday, Saturday. Saturday to Sunday.
Em                             |                          |
Get, get, get, get, get with us. You know what we say, say:
C                         |
Party every day. P-P-P - Party every day.
```

Chorus 2

```
                    ‖G          |
And I'm feel - ing
                    |C                    |
That tonight's    gonna be a good    night,
                    |Em                   |
That tonight's    gonna be a good    night,
                    |C                    |
That tonight's    gonna be a good,   good night.
          |G          |
A feel - ing
                    |C                    |
That tonight's    gonna be a good    night,
                    |Em                   |
That tonight's    gonna be a good    night,
                    |C                    |        |G      ‖
That tonight's    gonna be a good,   good night.
```

I Saw Three Ships

Traditional

G   D7   Em   C

Verse 1

|G   D7 |G   D7
I saw three ships come sailing in,

|G |D7
On Christmas Day, on Christmas Day.

|Em   D7 |G   D7
I saw three ships come sailing in,

|G   Em |C   D7 G
On Christmas Day in the morn - ing.

Verse 2

‖G   D7 |G   D7
And what was in those ships all three?

|G |D7
On Christmas Day, on Christmas Day.

|Em   D7 |G   D7
And what was in those ships all three?

|G   Em |C   D7 G
On Christmas Day in the morn - ing.

Verse 3

‖G   D7 |G   D7
Our Saviour Christ and His la-dy.

|G |D7
On Christmas Day, on Christmas Day.

|Em   D7 |G   D7
Our Saviour Christ and His la-dy.

|G   Em |C   D7 G
On Christmas Day in the morn - ing.

Verse 4

```
 ‖G        D7            ‖G          D7
Pray, whither sailed those ships all three?

   ‖G                  ‖D7
On Christmas Day, on Christmas Day.

      ‖Em      D7         ‖G          D7
Pray, whither sailed those ships all three?

   ‖G        Em       ‖C    D7 G
On Christmas Day in the morn  -  ing.
```

Verse 5

```
    ‖G        D7 ‖G      D7
O, they sailed into Bethle-hem.

   ‖G                  ‖D7
On Christmas Day, on Christmas Day.

   ‖Em        D7 ‖G     D7
O, they sailed into Bethle-hem.

   ‖G        Em       ‖C    D7 G
On Christmas Day in the morn  -  ing.
```

Verse 6

```
    ‖G        D7     ‖G          D7
And all the bells on earth shall ring,

   ‖G                  ‖D7
On Christmas Day, on Christmas Day.

   ‖Em      D7        ‖G          D7
And all the bells on earth shall ring,

   ‖G        Em       ‖C    D7 G
On Christmas Day in the morn  -  ing.
```

If I Had a Hammer
(The Hammer Song)

Words and Music by Lee Hays and Pete Seeger

G   C   D7   Em

132   4   1113   321

Verse 1

|G |C |G |C
If I had a hammer,   I'd hammer in the morn - ing,

|G |C |D7 |
I'd hammer in the evening   all over this land,

|G | |Em |
I'd hammer out danger, I'd hammer out a warning,

|C   G |C   G |
I'd hammer out love be - tween my brothers and my sisters,

C   G|D7 |G |C |G |
All   over this land.

Verse 2

‖G |C   I'd ring it in the morn - ing,
If I had a bell, |G |C

|G |C |D7 |
I'd ring it in the evening   all over this land,

|G | |Em |
I'd ring out danger, I'd ring out a warning,

|C   G |C   G |
I'd ring out love be - tween my brothers and my sisters,

C   G|D7 |G |C |G |
All   over this land.

Verse 3

            ‖G |C |G |C

If I had a song,   I'd sing it in the morn - ing,

                     |G |C |D7 |

I'd sing it in the evening all over this land,

               |G | |Em |

I'd sing out danger, I'd sing out a warning,

             |C   G |C   G |

I'd sing out love be - tween my brothers and my sisters,

C   G|D7 |G |C |G |

All   over this land.

Verse 4

               ‖G |C |G |C

Well, I've got a hammer   and I've got a bell,

             |G |C |D7 |

And I've got a song to sing all over this land,

                |G | |Em |

It's the hammer of justice, it's the bell of freedom,

            |C   G |C   G |

It's the song about love be - tween my brothers and my sisters,

C   G|D7 |G |C |G | ‖

All   over this land.

If I Were a Carpenter

Words and Music by
Tim Hardin

D   C   G

Verse 1

D   ‖C |
   If I were a carpenter

G |D |
   And you were a lady,

D |C |
   Would you marry me anyway,

G |D | |
   Would you have my baby?

D |C |
   If a tinker were my trade,

G |D |
   Would you still find me,

D |C |
   Carrying the pots I'd made,

G |D | |C   G |D   ‖
   Following be - hind me?

Bridge

C |D |
Save my love through loneliness,

C |D |
Save my love for sorrow

D |C |
   I've given you my ownliness;

G |D | | |
   Come and give me your to - morrow.

Verse 2

```
     D              ‖C                |
       If I worked my hands in wood
     G                |D             |
         Would you still love me?
     D                      |C              |
       Answer me, babe, "Yes, I would,
     G                |D            |              |
         I'd put you a - bove me."
     D           |C         |
       If I were a miller
     G                    |D              |
         At a mill wheel grinding,
     D                         |C                |
       Would you miss your colored blouse,
     G                |D          |          |C    G    |D              ‖
         Your soft shoes shining?
```

Interlude

```
     C        |G        |D        |          |C        |G        |D         |
```

Verse 3

```
     D              ‖C            |
       If I were a carpenter
     G                   |D        |
         And you were a lady,
     D                       |C        |
       Would you marry me anyway,
     G                       |D        |        |        |        |
         Would you have my baby?
     D                       |C        |
       Would you marry me anyway,
     G                       |D        |        |C    |G    |D        |        ‖
         Would you have my baby?
```

Jamaica Farewell

Words and Music by Irving Burgie

D   G   A7

1 2 3   1 3 2   1

Verse 1

D |G
Down the way where the nights are gay

|A7 |D |
And the moon shines gaily on the mountaintop,

D |G
I took a trip on a sailing ship,

|A7 |D
And when I reached Jamaica, I made a stop.

Chorus

||D |G |
But I'm sad to say, I'm on my way,

A7 |D
Won't be back for many a day.

|D |G
My heart is down, my head is turning around.

|A7 |D |
I had to leave a little crab in Kingston town.

G |A7 |D ||

Verse 2

```
        D                 |G
     Sounds of laughter everywhere,

        |A7              |D        |
  And the dancing fish swaying to and fro.

        D                 |G
     I must declare my heart is there,

          |A7              |D
  Though I've been from Maine to Mexico.
```

Repeat Chorus

Verse 3

```
        D                 |G              |
     Under the sea there you can hear Mer folk

   A7              |D        |
  Singing songs that I love so dear.

        D             |G           |A7
     Fish are dancing everywhere and the fun is fine

        |D
  Any time of year.
```

Repeat Chorus

Just the Way You Are

Words and Music by
Bruno Mars, Ari Levine, Philip Lawrence, Khari Cain and Khalil Walton

F   Dm7   B♭maj9

Intro

F | |Dm7 |
Ah,

|B♭maj9 | |F |
Ah,   ah.

Verse 1

||F
Oh, her eyes, her eyes
|F |
Make the stars look like they're not shining.
Dm7
Her hair, her hair
|Dm7 |
Falls perfectly without her trying.
B♭maj9 |
She's so beautiful,
|F | |
And I tell her every   day.   Yeah.

F
I know, I know
|F |
When I compliment her, she won't believe me.
Dm7
And it's so, it's so
|Dm7 |
Sad to think that she don't see what I see.
B♭maj9 | |F |
But every time she asks me, "Do I look okay?" I say:

Chorus 1

```
                          ‖F              |
When I see your face,
                    |Dm7                      |
There's not a thing    that I would change,
                    |B♭maj9          |              |F          |
'Cause you're amaz    -    ing just  the way you are.
                    |F          |
And when you smile,
                    |Dm7                    |
The whole world stops    and stares for a while,
                    |B♭maj9        |          |F      |        ‖
'Cause, girl, you're amaz   -   ing just  the way you are.          Yeah.
```

Verse 2

```
        F
    Her lips, her lips,
       |F                          |
I could kiss them all day if she'd let me.
Dm7
    Her laugh, her laugh,
    |Dm7                    |
She hates but I think it's so sexy.
B♭maj9              |
    She's so beautiful,
            |F        |
And I tell her every  day.
        |F
Oh, you know, you know, you know
        |F
I'd never ask you to change.
    |Dm7
If perfect's what you're searching for
        |Dm7
Then just stay the same.
    |B♭maj9                  |
So      don't even bother asking if   you look okay.
            |F        |
You know I'll say:
```

Chorus 2

                                  ‖F |

When I see your face,

                              |Dm7 |

There's not a thing   that I would change,

                         |B♭maj9 | **|F** |

'Cause you're amaz   -   ing just the way you are.

                              |F |

And when you smile,

                              |Dm7 |

The whole world stops   and stares for a while,

                         |B♭maj9 | **|F** |

'Cause, girl, you're amaz   -   ing just the way you are,

F | |

   The way you are,

F   **|Dm7** |

   The way you are.

                     |B♭maj9 | **|F** |

Girl, your amaz   -   ing just the way you are.

Repeat Chorus 1

Knockin' on Heaven's Door

Words and Music by
Bob Dylan

G   D   Am   C

Verse 1

G   D |Am
Mama, take   this badge from me.

G   D |C
I can't use   it any more.

G   D |Am
It's gettin' dark,   too dark to see.

G   D |C
Feels like I'm knockin' on heaven's door.

Chorus

G   D |C
Knock, knock, knockin' on heaven's door.

G   D |C
Knock, knock, knockin' on heaven's door.

G   D |C
Knock, knock, knockin' on heaven's door.

G   D |C
Knock, knock, knockin' on heaven's door.

Verse 2

G   D |Am
Mama, put   my guns in the ground.

G   D |C
I can't shoot   them any more.

G   D |Am
That cold black cloud is comin' down.

G   D |C
Feels like I'm knockin' on heaven's door.

Repeat Chorus (2x)

Kiss the Girl
from Walt Disney's THE LITTLE MERMAID

Music by Alan Menken
Lyrics by Howard Ashman

B   E   F#

3 2 1 1   2 3 4 1   3 1 2 1

Intro

B | | | ||

Verse 1

B | |
There you see her,

B | |
Sitting there across the way.

E | |B |
She don't got a lot to say,   but there's something a-bout her.

    |F# |E
And you don't know why, but you're dying to try.

    |B | ||
You wanna kiss the girl.

Verse 2

B | |
Yes, you want her.

B |
Look at her; you know you do.

    |E | |B |
It's possible she wants you, too. There's one way to ask her.

    |F# |E
It don't take a word, not a single word.

    |B | ||
Go on and kiss the girl.

Chorus 1

   B |E
  Sha la la la la la, my, oh, my.
              |B
Look at the boy, too shy.
          |F♯ |
Ain't gonna kiss the girl.
B |E
  Sha la la la la la, ain't it sad.
       |F♯
Ain't it a shame, too bad.
        |B | ||
You gonna miss the girl.

Verse 3

B | |
Now's your mo - ment,
B | |
Floating in a blue lagoon.
E |
Boy, you better do it soon;
        |B |
Time will be better.
     |F♯ |E
She won't   say a word and she won't say a word
     |B | ||
Until you kiss the girl.

Repeat Chorus 1

Interlude   B |E |B |F♯ |

                   B |E |F♯ |B ||

Chorus 2

B |E

  Sha la la la la la, don't be scared.

            |B

You got the mood prepared;

          |F♯ |

Go on and kiss the girl.

B |E

  Sha la la la la la, don't stop now.

          |F♯

Don't try to   hide it how

        |B ||

You wanna kiss the girl.

Chorus 3

B |E

  Sha la la la la la, float along

         |B

And listen to the song;

            |F♯ |

The song says, "Kiss the girl."

B |E

  Sha la la la la la, music play.

         |F♯

Do what the   music say.

        |B ||

You wanna kiss the girl.

Outro

B |E
You've got to kiss the girl.

B |F♯
Oh, won't you   kiss the girl.

B |E
You've got to kiss the girl.

F♯ |B
(Kiss the girl), kiss the girl, (kiss the girl).

B |E
You've got to kiss the girl.

B |F♯
You've got to kiss the girl.

B |E
Woh, kiss the girl.

F♯ |B
(Kiss the girl), kiss the girl, (kiss the girl).

Knock Three Times

Words and Music by
Irwin Levine and Larry Russell Brown

D   A7   G   D7

Verse 1

D
Hey, girl, what ya do-in' down there?

D   **A7**
Dancin' alone every night while I live right a-bove you.

A7
I can hear your music play-in',

A7
I can feel your body sway-in',

A7   **D**
One floor below me, you don't even know me, I love you.

Chorus

G   **D**
Oh, my darlin', knock three times on the ceiling if you want me,

A7   **D** **D7**
Twice on the pipe if the answer is no.

G   **D**
Oh, my sweetness, *(3 knocks)* means you'll meet me in the hallway,

A7   **D** **G A7**
Twice on the pipe means you ain't gonna show.

Verse 2   ‖**D** | |
If you look out your win-dow tonight,

D | |**A7** | |
Pull in the string with the note that's attached to my heart.

A7 |
Read how many times I saw you,

|**A7** |
How in my silence I adore you,

|**A7** | |**D**
And only in my dreams did that wall between us come a-part.

Repeat Chorus (2X)

Kum Ba Yah

Traditional Spiritual

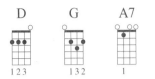

Verse 1

           |D   G |D
Kum - bah - yah, my Lord,   Kum - bah - yah,

           |D   G   D |A7
Kum - bah - yah, my Lord,   Kum - bah - yah,

D | G |D
Kum - bah - yah, my Lord,   Kum - bah - yah,

A7 |D   A7 |D
Oh, Lord,   Kum - bah - yah.

Verse 2

          ||D   G |D
Someone's prayin', Lord,   Kum - bah - yah,

           |D   G   D |A7
Someone's prayin', Lord,   Kum - bah - yah,

D | G |D
Someone's prayin', Lord,   Kum - bah - yah,

A7 |D   A7 |D
Oh, Lord,   Kum - bah - yah.

Verse 3

          ||D   G |D
Someone's singin', Lord,   Kum - bah - yah,

           |D   G   D |A7
Someone's singin', Lord,   Kum - bah - yah,

D | G |D
Someone's singin', Lord,   Kum - bah - yah,

A7 |D   A7 |D ||
Oh, Lord,   Kum - bah - yah.

Lookin' Out My Back Door

Words and Music by John Fogerty

G   Em   C   D
1 3 2   3 2 1   4   1 2 3

Verse 1

G | |
Just got home from Illinois.

Em | |
Lock the front door, oh boy!

C |**G** |**D** |
Got to sit down, take a rest on the porch.

|**G** | |
I - magination sets in.

Em | |
Pretty soon I'm singin'.

C |**G** |**D** |**G**
Doo, doo, doo, lookin' out my back door.

Verse 2

```
    ‖G              |
There's a giant doing cartwheels,

 |Em            |           |
A statue wearin' high heels.

C          |G           |D          |
Look at all the happy creatures dancing on the lawn.

 |G            |          |
A dinosaur Vic - trola

Em             |          |
Listening to Buck Owens.

C        |G       |D       |G         ‖
Doo, doo, doo, lookin' out my back door.
```

Chorus 1

```
D                    |
Tambourines and elephants

 |C          |G
Are playing in the band.

       |G         |Em       |D      |                |
Won't you take a ride   on the flyin' spoon? Doo, doo doo.

G            |
Wondrous appa - rition

     |Em         |          |
Pro - vided by ma - gician.

C        |G       |D       |G         ‖
Doo, doo, doo, lookin' out my back door.
```

Chorus 2

D |
Tambourines and elephants

     |C   **|G**
Are playing in the band.

        |G   **|Em**   **|D** | |
Won't you take a ride   on the flyin' spoon?   Doo, doo doo.

G |
Bother me to - morrow.

    |Em | |
To - day, I'll buy no sorrows.

C   **|G**   **|D**   **|G** ||
Doo, doo, doo, lookin' out my back door.

G | |

Verse 3

Forward troubles Illinois.

Em | |
Lock the front door, oh boy!

C   **|G**   **|D** | |
Look at all the happy creatures dancing on the lawn.

G |
Bother me to - morrow.

   |Em | |
To - day, I'll buy no sorrows.

C   **|G**   **|D**   **|G** ||
Doo, doo, doo, lookin' out my back door.

Leaving on a Jet Plane

Words and Music by
John Denver

G   C   D

Verse 1

|G |C
All my bags are packed, I'm ready to go,

|G |C
I'm standing here out-side your door,

|G |C |D |
I hate to wake you up to say good-bye.

|G |C
But the dawn is breakin', it's early morn,

|G |C
The taxi's waitin', he's blowin' his horn,

|G |C |D |
Al-ready I'm so lonesome I could die.

Chorus

‖G |C |
So kiss me and smile for me,

G |C |
Tell me that you'll wait for me,

G |C |D |
Hold me like you'll never let me go.

|G C |G
'Cause I'm leavin' on a jet plane,

|C |G
Don't know when I'll be back again.

|C |D | | |
Oh, babe, I hate to go.

Verse 2

     ||G |C
There's so many times I've let you down,

   |G |C
So many times I've played around,

   |G |C |D |
I tell you now they don't mean a thing.

    |G |C
Every place I go I'll think of you,

    |G |C
Every song I sing I'll sing for you,

    |G |C |D |
When I come back I'll bring your wedding ring.

Repeat Chorus

Verse 3

 G |C |
Now the time has come to leave you,

 G |C
One more time let me kiss you,

   |G |C |D | |
Then close your eyes, I'll be on my way.

 G |C
Dream about the days to come

   |G |C
When I won't have to leave alone,

  |G |C |D | ||
A-bout the times I won't have to say:

Repeat Chorus

Outro

   |G |C |G
I'm leavin' on a jet plane,

     |C |G
Don't know when I'll be back again,

   |C | |D | | | | | |G ||
Oh, babe, I hate to go.

Let's Get Together
(Get Together)

Words and Music by
Chet Powers

D   C   G   A

1 2 3   4   1 3 2   2 1

Verse 1

D | | |C | |
Love is but a song we sing, fear's the way we die.

D | | |C | |
You can make the mountains ring or make the angels cry.

D | | |C | ||
Though the bird is on the wing and you may not know why…

Chorus

G |A
Come on people now,   smile on your brother.

     |D |G   A |D | ||
Every-body get together, try to love one an-other right now.

Verse 2

D | | |C | |
Some may come and some may go, we shall surely pass

D | | |C | |
When the one that left us here returns for us at last.

D | | |C | ||
We are but a moment's sunlight fading in the grass.

Repeat Chorus (2X)

Verse 3

```
D                    |           |       |C    |      |
  If you hear the song I sing, we will under-stand.

D                      |           |              |C    |      |
  You hold the key to love and fear all in your trembling hand.

D                    |           |              |C    |    ||
  Just one key un-locks them both, it's there at your com-mand.
```

Repeat Chorus

Outro-Chorus

```
G                        |A
  Come on people now,   smile on your brother.

      |D                   |G       A      |D
  Every-body get together, try to love one an-other right now,

      |D        |     |     ||
  Right now, right now.
```

Louisiana Bayou

Words and Music by
Dave Matthews Band and Mark Batson

Verse 1

A

No, no, Mama cried devil; they do - si - do.

A

Two young boys lyin' dead by the side of the road.

A

The coins on their eyes represent the mon - ey they owe.

A

No judge or jury ever gonna hear the story told.

Chorus 1

‖A

Down by the bayou,

|A

Try'n' to play with the cane, you, ah.

|A

Try'n' to play with the cane, you, ah.

|A

Same story again, you, ah.

|A

Down by the bayou,

|A

Try'n' to play with the cane, you, ah.

|A

Try'n' to play with the cane, you, ah.

|A

Same story again, you.

|A

Louisiana Bayou.

Verse 2

    A | |

   Sweet girl, Daddy done beat that girl like he's insane.

    A | |

   Brother can't watch him beat that girl down again.

    A | |

   Till late one night cookin' up with a cou - ple of friends,

    A |

   Swears his daddy never gonna see an - other day.

Chorus 2

               ‖ **A**

Down by the bayou,

                   | **A**

Try'n' to play with the cane, you, ah.

                   | **A**

Try'n' to play with the cane, you, ah.

            | **A**

Same story again, you, ah.

           | **A**

Down by the bayou,

                  | **A**

Try'n' to play with the cane, you, ah.

                  | **A**

Try'n' to play with the cane, you, ah.

            | **A**

Same story again, you, ah.

Bridge

||**A** | |
Bring the same. No, no, Mama cried devil; they do - si - do.

A |
  See two young boys lyin' dead by the side of the road.

      |**A**   **Dm**
Shame, shame.

  |**Dm**   **A** | |
Oh, it's a shame to lose your   way running wild.

A |
It's a shame to lose your… Shame, shame.

Dm | **A** | |
Oh, it's a shame to lose your way as a child.   Oh, oh,

A ||
   It's a shame to lose your…

Verse 3

A | |
  Money on the bed but you ain't got to go.

A | |
  Sold your soul, just try'n' to get o - verload.

A | |
  No empty pocket gonna keep you from get - tin' yours.

A |
  No judge or jury ever gonna hear the story told.

Repeat Chorus 2

A
    No, no, Mama cried devil; they do - si - do.

A
   Two young boys lyin' dead by the side of the road.

|**A**
Down by the bayou,

|**A**
Try'n' to play with the cane, you, ah.

|**A**
Try'n' to play with the cane, you, ah.

|**A**
Same story again, you, ah.

|**A**
Down by the bayou,

Dm
Try'n' to play with the cane, you, ah.

A
Try'n' to play with the cane, you, ah.

A
Same story again, you, ah.

|**A**
Down by the bayou,

|**A**
Louisiana Bayou.

|**A**
Louisiana Bayou.

Man of Constant Sorrow

Traditional

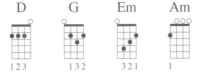

D   G   Em   Am

Verse 1

|**D** | |**G** |
I am a man   of constant sorrow,

|**Em** | |**Am** |
I've seen trou - ble all my days.

|**D** | |**G** |
I bid fare - well   to old Ken - tucky,

|**Em** | |**Am** |
The place where I   was born and raised.

Verse 2

||**D** | |**G** |
For six long years I've been in trouble,

|**Em** | |**Am** |
No pleasure here   on earth I've found.

|**D** | |**G** |
For in this world   I'm bound to ramble,

|**Em** | |**Am** |
I have no friends   to help me now.

Verse 3

          ‖**D** | **|G** |
It's fare you well,   my own true lover,

          |**Em** | |**Am** |
I never ex - pect   to see you a - gain.

          |**D** | |**G** |
For I'm bound to ride   that northern railroad,

          |**Em** | |**Am** |
Perhaps I'll die   upon this train.

Verse 4

          ‖**D** | **|G** |
You can bury me   in some deep valley,

          |**Em** | |**Am** |
For many years   where I may lay,

          |**D** | |**G** |
Then you may learn   to love an - other,

          |**Em** | |**Am** |
While I am sleep - ing in my grave.

Verse 5

          ‖**D** | **|G** |
Maybe your friends   think I'm just a stranger,

          |**Em** | |**Am** |
My face you nev - er will see no more,

          |**D** | |**G** |
But there is one   promise that is given,

          |**Em** | |**Am** | ‖
I'll meet you on   God's golden shore.

Me and Bobby McGee

Words and Music by
Kris Kristofferson and Fred Foster

C   G7   C7   F

Verse 1

C
Busted flat in Baton Rouge,   headin' for the trains,

C |G7
Feelin' nearly faded as my jeans.

G7
    Bobby thumbed a diesel down   just before it rained,

G7 |C
    Took us all the way to New Orleans.

C
I took my har - poon out of my dirty red ban - dana

    |C |C7 |F
And was blowin' sad while Bobby sang the blues.

    |F |C
With them windshield wipers slappin' time and Bobby clappin' hands,

    |G7 |C
We finally sang up every song that driver knew.

Chorus 1

F |C
    Freedom's just an - other word for nothin' left to lose.

G7 |C
    Nothin' ain't worth nothin', but it's free.

F |C
    Feelin' good was easy, Lord, when   Bobby sang the blues,

G7
    And feelin' good was good enough for me,

G7 |C
    Good enough for me and Bobby Mc - Gee.

Verse 2

‖**C** | | | |
From the coal mines of Ken - tucky   to the California sun,

C | |**G7** | |
Bobby shared the secrets of my soul.

G7 | | | |
    Standin' right be - side me, Lord, through   everything I done,

G7 | |**C** |
    And every night she kept me from the cold.

|**C** | | | |
Then somewhere near Sa - linas, Lord, I let her slip a - way,

C |**C7** |**F** |
Lookin' for the home I hope she'll find.

|**F** | |**C** | |
And I'd trade all of my to - morrows for a single yester - day,

G7 | |**C** | ‖
Holdin' Bobby's body next to mine.

Chorus 2

F | |**C** | |
    Freedom's just an - other word for nothin' left to lose.

G7 | |**C** | |
    Nothin' left is all she left for me.

F | |**C** | |
    Feelin' good was easy, Lord, when   Bobby sang the blues,

G7 | | | |
  And, buddy, that was good enough for me,

G7 | |**C** | ‖
    Good enough for me and Bobby Mc - Gee.

MMM Bop

Words and Music by
Isaac Hanson, Taylor Hanson and Zac Hanson

A   E   D

Verse 1

A   E |D
You have so many re‑lationships in this life,

     E |A
Only one or two will last.

             E |D
You're going through all this pain and strife,

             E |A E
Then you turn your back and they're gone so fast,

     |D E |A   E |D E ||
Ooh yeah, and they're gone so fast.

Verse 2

A   E |D
So hold on to the ones who really care,

     E |A
In the end they'll be the only ones there. |

           E   D
When you get old and start losing your hair,

     E |A   E |D
Can you tell me who will still care?

     E |A   E |D E ||
Can you tell me who will still care? Oh, oh, yeah, yeah.

Chorus

A |D
Mmm bop, ba du‑ba dop, ba du bop, ba du‑ba dop.

|A   E |
Ba du bop, ba du‑ba dop, ba du, yah‑ee, yeah.

A |D
Mmm bop, ba du‑ba dop, ba du bop, ba du‑ba dop.

|A   E ||
Ba du bop, ba du‑ba dop, ba du, yah‑ee, yeah.

Verse 3

A   E |D
Plant a seed, plant a flower, plant a rose.

        E |A
You can plant any one of those.

       E |D
Keep planting to find out which one grows.

      E |A   E |D
It's a secret no one knows,

      E |A   E |D E ||
It's a secret no one knows,   no one knows.

Repeat Chorus

Bridge

A   E |D E |A
In an mmm bop they're gone, in an mmm bop they're not there.

      E |D E |A E |D
In an mmm bop they're gone, in an mmm bop they're not there

    E |A E |D   E ||
Un - til you lose your hair, uh huh, but you don't care, mmm yeah, yeah.

Repeat Chorus

Outro

A   E |D   E |A
Can you tell me? Uh, you know you can, but you don't know.

     E |D   E |A
Can you tell me? Oh yeah, you say you can, but you don't know.

     E |D   E |A
Can you tell me? Ah, you know you can, but you don't know.

     E |D   E |A E |D
Can you tell me? You say you can, but you don't know.

     E |A
You say you can, but you don't know,

E |D   E ||
You don't know, you don't know.

Repeat Chorus

Mr. Tambourine Man

Words and Music by
Bob Dylan

G   A   D

132 21   123

Chorus

   G |A |D |G
Hey, Mister Tam - bourine Man, play a song for me;
      |D |G |A | |
I'm not sleepy and there ain't no place I'm goin' to.
   G |A |D |G
Hey, Mister Tam - bourine Man, play a song for me;
      |D |G |A |D | ||
In the jingle jangle morning I'll come followin' you.

Verse

   G |A |D |G
Take me for a trip upon your magic swirlin' ship.
      |D |G
All my senses have been stripped
         |D |G
And my hands can't feel to grip
      |D |G
And my toes too numb to step;
    |D |G |A |
Wait only for my boot heels to be wanderin'.
     |G |A |D |G
I'm ready to go anywhere, I'm ready for to fade
      |D |G
On - to my own pa - rade.
        |D |G
Cast your dancing spell my way;
   |G |A | ||
I promise to go under it.

Repeat Chorus

Ode to Billy Joe

Words and Music by
Bobbie Gentry

D7   G7   C7

1 1 1 3   2 1 3   1

Verse 1

           |D7
It was the third of June,
      |D7 | |
Another sleepy, dusty Delta day.
     |D7
I was out choppin' cotton
     |D7 | |
And my brother was balin' hay.
      |G7
And at dinner time we stopped
       |G7 | |
And walked back to the house to eat,
      |D7
And Mama hollered out the back door,
     |D7 | |
"Y'all re - member to wipe your feet."
      |G7 |
And then she said, "I got some news this morn - in'
           |G7 |
From Choctaw Ridge.
    |D7
Today Billy Joe McAllister
    |C7   **|D7** |
Jumped off the Tallahatchie Bridge."

Verse 2

    ‖**D7**
And Papa said to Mama
    |**D7** | |
As he passed around the black-eyed peas,
               |**D7** |
"Well, Billy Joe   never had a lick o' sense.
D7 | |
    Pass the biscuits, please.
    |**G7**
There's five more acres
    |**G7** | |
In the lower forty I've got to plow."
       |**D7**
And Mama said it was shame
    |**D7** | |
About   Billy Joe, anyhow.
     |**G7**
Seems like nothin' ever comes
     |**G7** | |
To no good up on Choctaw Ridge.
    |**D7**
And now Billy Joe McAllister's
   |**C7** |**D7** |
Jumped off the Tallahatchie Bridge.

Verse 3

|| **D7**
And Brother said he recollected

| **D7** | |
When he and Tom and Billie Joe

| **D7**
Put a frog down my back

| **D7** | |
At the Carroll County picture show.

| **G7**
And wasn't I talkin' to him

| **G7** | |
After church last Sunday night?

| **D7** |
I'll have an - other piece of apple pie.

D7 | |
You know, it don't seem right.

| **G7** |
I saw him at the sawmill yester - day

| **G7** |
On Choctaw Ridge.

| **D7**
And now you tell me Billie Joe's

| **C7** | **D7** | ||
Jumped off the Tallahatchie Bridge.

Verse 4

D7
Mama said to me,
        D7
"Child, what's happened to your appetite?
      D7
I've been cookin' all morning
      D7
And you haven't touched a single bite.
   G7
That nice young preacher,
     G7
Brother Taylor, dropped by today.
       D7
Said he'd be pleased to have dinner
  D7
On Sunday. Oh, by the way,
   G7
He said he saw a girl that looked a lot like you
         G7
Up on Choctaw Ridge,
      D7
And she and Billy Joe was throwing
   C7   **D7**
Somethin' off the Tallahatchie Bridge."

Verse 5

|D7
A year has come and gone
|D7 | |
Since we heard the news 'bout Billy Joe.
|D7
And Brother married Becky Thompson;
|D7 | |
They bought a store in Tupelo.
|G7
There was a virus goin' 'round,
|G7 | |
Papa caught it and he died last spring.
|D7
And now Mama doesn't seem
|D7 | |
To wanna do much of anything.
|G7 |
And me, I spend a lot of time pickin' flowers up
|G7 |
On Choctaw Ridge
|D7 |
And drop them into the muddy water
C7 |D7 | | | ||
Off the Tallahatchie Bridge.

My Generation

Words and Music by
Peter Townshend

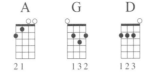

Intro A |G |A |G ||

Verse 1

A |G |
People try to put us d - down.

A   D |G |
(Talkin' 'bout my generation.)

A |G |
  Just because we   get around.

A   D |G |
(Talkin' 'bout my generation.)

A |G |
Things they do look awful c - c - cold.

A   D |G |
(Talkin' 'bout my generation.)

|A |G |
I hope I die before I get old.

A   D |G |
(Talkin' 'bout my generation.)

|A |G
This is my gener - ation.

|A |G ||
This is my gener - ation, baby.

Verse 2

A |G |
Why don't you all f - fade away?

A   D |G |
(Talkin' 'bout my generation.)

A |G |
Don't try to dig what we all s - s - say.

A   D |G
(Talkin' 'bout my generation.)

   |A |G |A
I'm not tryin' to cause a big s - s - sensa - tion.

          D |G
(Talkin' 'bout my generation.)

   |A |G |A
I'm just talkin' 'bout my g - g - g - gener - ation.

          D |G
(Talkin' 'bout my generation.)

          |A |G
This is my gener - ation.

          |A |G ||
This is my gener - ation, baby.

Repeat Verse 1

My Ramblin' Boy

Words and Music by Tom Paxton

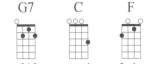

Verse 1

       |**G7** |**C**
He was a man and a friend al - ways,

         |**G7** |**C**
He stuck with me in the hard old days.

     |**C** |
He never cared if I had no dough,

       |**G7** |**C**
We rambled 'round in the rain and snow.

Chorus

       ‖**C**   **F** |**C**
And here's to you my ramblin' boy,

    |**G7** |**C**
May all your ramblin' bring you joy.

    |**C**   **F** |**C**
And here's to you my ramblin' boy,

    |**G7** |**C**
May all your ramblin' bring you joy.

Verse 2

```
         ‖G7                    |C
In Tulsa town we chanced to stray.

            |G7              |C
We thought we'd try to work one day.

             |C                   |
The boss said he had room for one.

          |G7              |C
Says my old pal, "We'd rather bum!"
```

Repeat Chorus

Verse 3

```
          ‖G7                |C
Late one night in a jungle camp,

            |G7              |C
The weather it was cold and damp.

          |C                     |
He got the chills and he got 'em bad;

           |G7            |C       ‖
They took the only friend I had.
```

Repeat Chorus

Verse 4

```
          ‖G7             |C
He left me there to ramble on,

           |G7                |C
My ramblin' pal is dead and gone.

          |C                   |
If when we die, we go some - where,

            |G7              |C    ‖
I'll bet you a dollar, he's ramblin' there.
```

Repeat Chorus

Oh! Susanna

Words and Music by Stephen C. Foster

C   D7   G7   F

Verse

|C | |D7 |G7
I come from Ala - bama with a banjo on my knee.

|C | |G7 |C
I'm goin' to Lou'si - ana, my Su - sanna for to see.

|C | |D7 |G7
It rained all night the day I left, the weather it was dry.

|C | |G7 |C ||
The sun so hot I froze to death. Su - sanna, don't you cry.

Chorus

F | |C   D7 |G7
Oh, Su - sanna, oh don't you cry for me,

|C | |G7 |C ||
For I come from Ala - bama with a banjo on my knee.

Rodeo Clowns

Words and Music by Jack Johnson

Em   A   C   B

Verse 1

Em
Sweeping the floors, open up the doors, yeah.

A
Turn on the lights, getting ready for tonight.

C
Nobody's romancing 'cause it's too early for dancing,

|**B**
But here comes the music.

Verse 2

Em
Bright lights flashing to cover up your lack of soul.

|**A**
Man - y people, so many problems,

|**C**
So many reasons to buy an - other round; drink it down.

|**B**
Just another night on the town

|**Em**
With the big man, money man, better than the other man.

A
He got the plan with the million dollar give a damn.

C
When nobody understands he'll become a smaller man.

|**B**
The bright lights keep flashing.

Chorus

                                               ||**Em**   **B**
Women keep on dancing with the clowns, yeah, yeah, yeah.

                                         |**C**   **A**
They pick me up when I'm down,   yeah, yeah.

                     |**Em**   **B**
The rodeo clowns,   yeah, yeah, yeah,

                                 |**C**   **A** ||
They pick me up when I'm down.

Verse 3

        ||**Em**
The disco ball spinning,

                                       |**A**
All the music and the women and the shots of tequila.

Man, they say that they need ya.

  |**C**
But what they really need

    |**B**
Is just a little room to breathe.

     |**Em**
Teeny bopping disco queen,

                           |**A**
She barely understands her dreams   of bellybutton rings

                   |**C**
And other kinds of things sym - bolic of change.

But the thing that is strange

    |**B**
Is that the changes occurred.

Chorus

                                           ‖**Em**   **B**
And now she's just a part of the herd,   yeah, yeah, yeah.

                                |**C**   **A**
Man, I thought that you heard, yeah, yeah.

                    |**Em**   **B**
The changes occurred,   yeah, yeah, yeah.

                  |**C**   **A**   ‖
Just a part of the herd.

Verse 4

Em
Lights out, shut down, late night, wet ground. |

A |
 You walk by, look at him, but he can't look at you, yeah.

C |
 You might feel pity, but he only feels the ground.

B |
 You understand moods, but he only knows letdown.

Em |
  By the corner there's another one

A |
Reaching out a hand, coming from a broken man.

    |**C** |**B**
Well,   you try to live, but he's done trying.   Not dead,

Chorus

                  ‖**Em**
But definitely dying

B |**C**   **A**
 With the rest of the clowns,   yeah, yeah.

                          |**Em**   **B**
Mm, mm, mm, mm,   mm, mm, mm,

                               |**C**   **A**   ‖
With the rest of the clowns.

Repeat Verse 1

Ring of Fire

Words and Music by
Merle Kilgore and June Carter

A   D   E7

Verse 1

A | D |A |D   A |
Love   is a burning thing

        |A | E7 |A |E7   A | |
And it makes   a fiery ring.

A | D |A |D   A | |
Bound   by wild de - sires,

A |E7 |A | ||
I fell into a ring of fire.

Chorus

E7 | |D |A
I   fell   in -   to a burning ring of fire.

     |E7 | |D |A
I went down,   down,   down,   and the flames   went   higher.

    |A | | E7   A |
And it burns,   burns,   burns,   the ring of fire,

E7 |A |
The ring of fire.

Verse 2

||A | D |A |D |A |
The taste   of love is sweet

   |A | E7 |A |E7 |A | |
When hearts   like ours meet.

A |D |A | |D |A | |
I fell for you like a child

A | E7 |A | ||
Oh,   but the fire went wild.

Repeat Chorus

Tag

    ||A | | E7 |A |
And it burns, burns, burns, the ring of fire,

    E7 |A | E7 |A ||
The ring of fire,   the ring of fire.

Runaround Sue

Words and Music by
Ernie Marasca and Dion Di Mucci

```
   D        Bm        G         A
 ┌─┬─┬─┐  ┌─┬─┬─┐  ┌─┬─┬─┐  ┌─┬─┬─┐
 │ │ │●  ●─●─●─●  ●│ │ │  ●│ │●●
 │ │●│●  │ │●│●  │ │●●│  │●│ │ │
 │●│ │ │  │ │ │●  │ │ │ │  │ │ │ │
 ───────  ───────  ───────  ───────
  1 2 3    3 1 1 1   1 3 2    2 1
```

Intro

    D | |
    Here's my story, it's sad but true;
Bm | |
    It's about a girl that I once knew.
G | |
    She took my love then ran around
A | ||
    With every single guy in town.

Chorus 1

D | |
(Hayp hayp   bumda hady hady,
Bm | |
Hayp hayp   bumda hady hady,
G | **A** | |
Hayp hayp   bumda hady hady hayp.
D | |
Hayp hayp   bumda hady hady,
Bm | |
Hayp hayp   bumda hady hady,
G | **A** **N.C.** | ||
Hayp hayp   bumda hady hady hayp. Ah.)

Verse 1

```
         D                              |              |
         I should have known it from the very start,
       Bm                          |              |
         This girl would leave me with a broken heart.
       G                      |             |
         Now listen, people, what I'm telling you:
       A   N.C.              |            ||
         A-keep away from Runaround Sue.
```

Verse 2

```
         D                       |
         I miss her lips and the smile on her face,
         |Bm                    |              |
       The touch of her hair and this girl's warm embrace.
       G                     |          |
         So if you don't wanna cry  like I do,
       A   N.C.              |            ||
         A-keep away from Runaround Sue.
```

Chorus 2

```
         D           |              |
       (Hayp hayp  bumda hady hady,
       Bm        |            |
       Hayp hayp   bumda hady hady,
       G         |            |A   N.C.|        ||
       Hayp hayp   bumda hady hady hayp. Ah.)
```

Bridge 1

G

She likes to travel around;

                D

Yeah, she'll love you and she'll put you down.

    G

Now people, let me put you wise:

A   **N.C.**

Sue goes out with other guys.

Verse 3

            D

Here's the moral and the story from the guy who knows;

Bm

    I fell in love and my love still grows.

G

Ask any fool that she ever knew, they'll say:

A   **N.C.**

   A-keep away from Runaround Sue.

Chorus 3

D

(Hayp hayp.) Yeah, keep away from this girl.

Bm

(Hayp hayp.) I don't know what she'll do.

G   **A**   **N.C.**

(Hayp hayp.)   Keep away from Sue. (Ah.)

Bridge 2

```
           G                    |
She likes to travel around;
                  | D                       |
Yeah, she'll love you and she'll put you down.
     | G                        |           |
Now people, let me put you wise:
A    N.C.|
She goes out with other guys.
```

Repeat Verse 3

Chorus 4

```
           D              |                    |
(Hayp hayp.) Stay away from that girl.
Bm                   |                    |
(Hayp hayp.) Don't you know what she'll do now?
G             |              | A       |         | D        ||
(Hayp hayp   bumda hady hady hayp.)
```

Sexy Plexi

Words and Music by Jack Johnson

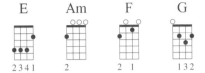

Verse 1

E |**Am** |
Sexy, sexy, made up of plexi dis - asters.

E |
Pushing and pulling, conservative rolling,

Am |
Unlike plastic, easier to see through,

E |
Just like glass with no ring,

Am |
Softer and sadder you sing.

E |
Sexy, sexy, do your thing,

Am |
Learn to be shy and then you can sting.

E |
Plexi, plexi, bend, don't shatter.

F   **G**   ‖
Once you're broken, shape won't matter.

Chorus

```
       Am                      G
       You're breaking your    mind

       |F                      E
By  killing the time that kills    you.

       |Am                          G
But  you  can't  blame  the  time,

                    |F              E       |Am       |        ‖
'Cause  it's  on - ly  in  your  mind.
```

Verse 2

```
       E
       Quickly, quickly grow and then you'll know

                   |Am
It's  such  an  awkward  show  to  see.

       |E
And  everyone  you  wanted  to  know

       |Am
And  everyone  you  wanted  to  meet

              |E          |Am
Have  all     gone  away.

                    |E              |F   G            ‖
Well,  they've  all     gone  away.        And now…
```

Repeat Chorus

Bridge

```
       Am                                  |E
       You're breaking your mind, you're    breaking your mind.

              |Am                          |E
You're      breaking your mind, you're    breaking your mind.

              |Am                          |E
You're      breaking your mind, you're    breaking your mind.

              |Am                          |E                          |F    G      ‖
You're      breaking your mind, you're    breaking your mind, mind,    mind.
```

Outro

```
       Am   G   |F   E   |Am   G   |F   E   |Am          ‖
```

113

Shelter from the Storm

Words and Music by Bob Dylan

D   A   G

Verse 1

D |A |G |D
'Twas in another lifetime, one of toil and blood,

|D |A |G | |
When blackness was a virtue and the road was full of mud.

D |A |G |
I came in from the wilderness, a creature void of form.

|D |A |G |D |A |G |D
"Come in," she said, "I'll give you shelter from the storm."

Verse 2

||D |A |G |D
And if I pass this way again, you can rest as - sured

|D |A |G |
I'll always do my best for her, on that I give my word,

|D |A |G |
In a world of steel-eyed death, and men who are fighting to be warm.

|D |A |G |D |A |G |D |
"Come in," she said, "I'll give you shelter from the storm."

Verse 3

    ‖**D** |**A** |**G** |**D** |
Not a word was spoke be - tween us; there was little risk in - volved.

D |**A** |**G** | |
Everything up to that point had been left unre - solved.

D |**A** |**G** |
Try imagin - ing a place where it's always safe and warm.

    |**D** |**A** |**G** |**D** |**A** |**G** |**D** |
"Come in," she said, "I'll give you shelter from the storm."

Verse 4

    ‖**D** |**A** |**G** |**D** |
I was burned out from ex - haustion, buried in the hail,

D |**A** |**G** | |
Poisoned in the bushes an' blown out on the trail,

D |**A** |**G** |
Hunted like a crocodile, ravaged in the corn.

    |**D** |**A** |**G** |**D** |**A** |**G** |**D** ‖
"Come in," she said, "I'll give you shelter from the storm."

Verse 5

D |**A** |**G** |**D**
Suddenly I turned around and she was standin' there

    |**D** |**A** |**G** |
With silver bracelets on her wrists and flowers in her hair.

    |**D** |**A** |**G** |
She walked up to me so gracefully and took my crown of thorns.

    |**D** |**A** |**G** |**D** |**A** |**G** |**D**
"Come in," she said, "I'll give you shelter from the storm."

Verse 6

    ‖**D** |**A** |**G** |**D**
Now there's a wall be - tween us; somethin' there's been lost.

    |**D** |**A** |**G** | |
I took too much for granted; I got my signals crossed.

D |**A** |**G** |
Just to think that it all began on a non-eventful morn.

    |**D** |**A** |**G** |**D** |**A** |**G** |**D**
"Come in," she said, "I'll give you shelter from the storm."

Verse 7

|‖D |A |G |D

Well, the deputy walks on hard nails and the preacher rides a mount,

|D |A |G |

But nothing really matters much; it's doom alone that counts.

|D |A |G |

And the one-eyed under - taker, he blows a futile horn.

|D |A |G |D |A |G |D   ‖

"Come in," she said, "I'll give you shelter from the storm."

Verse 8

D |A |G |D |

I've heard newborn babies wailin' like a mournin' dove

|D |A |G |

And old men with broken teeth stranded without love.

|D |A |G |

Do I understand your question, man? Is it hopeless and for - lorn?

|D |A |G |D |A |G |D

"Come in," she said, "I'll give you shelter from the storm."

Verse 9

|‖D |A |G |D

In a little hilltop village, they gambled for my clothes.

|D |A |G |

I bargained for sal - vation an' she gave me a lethal dose.

|D |A |G |

I offered up my innocence and got repaid with scorn.

|D |A |G |D |A |G |D

"Come in," she said, "I'll give you shelter from the storm."

Verse 10

|‖D |A |G |D |

Well, I'm livin' in a foreign country but I'm bound to cross the line.

D |A |G |

Beauty walks a razor's edge; some - day I'll make it mine.

|D |A |G |

If I could only turn back the clock to when God and her were born.

|D |A |G |D |A |G |D   ‖

"Come in," she said, "I'll give you shelter from the storm."

The Sound of Silence

Words and Music by
Paul Simon

Am   G   C   F

Intro

Am |

Verse 1

Am   ‖G |
   Hello, darkness, my old friend;
G |Am |
   I've come to talk with you a - gain,
Am   C |F   C |
   Because a vision softly   creeping
C |F   C |
   Left it's seeds while I was   sleeping,
C |F | |C
   And the vision that was planted in my brain
         |C   Am |C |G |Am |
Still re - mains   within the sound of silence.

Verse 2

Am   ‖G |
   In restless dreams I walked a - lone,
G |Am |
   Narrow streets of cobble - stone.
Am   C |F   C |
   'Neath the halo of a   streetlamp,
C |F   C |
   I turned my collar to the cold and damp,
C |F | |C
   When my eyes were stabbed by the flash of a neon light
         |C   Am |C |G |Am |
That split the night   and touched the sound of silence.

Verse 3

```
        Am                       ‖G          |
        And in the naked light I saw
        G                         |Am          |
        Ten thousand people, maybe more.
        Am       C          |F       C       |
        People talking without  speaking,
        C                    |F       C       |
        People hearing without  listening,
        C            |F       |            |C
        People writing songs that voices never share,
              |C  Am  |C        |G      |Am        |
        And no one dare       disturb the sound of silence.
```

Verse 4

```
        Am                           ‖G          |
        "Fools!" said I, "You do not know
        G                     |Am          |
        Silence like a cancer grows.
        Am       C            |F       C       |
        Hear my words that I might  teach you;
        C                        |F         C       |
        Take my arms that I might  reach you."
        C     |F       |            |C        |        Am
        But my words like silent raindrops fell,
          |C        |G  |Am        |
        And echoed in the wells of silence.
```

118

Verse 5

```
    Am                          ‖G          |
        And the people bowed and prayed
    G                      |Am          |
        To the neon god they made.
    Am        C              |F      C          |
        And the sign flashed out its  warning
    C                     |F      C          |
        In the words that it was   forming,
    C                          |F
        And the signs said, "The words of the prophets
        |F                    |C          |      Am
    Are written on the subway walls   and tenement halls"
        |C              |G    |Am      |          ‖
    And whispered in the sounds of silence.
```

Silent Night

Words by Joseph Mohr
Translated by John F. Young
Music by Franz X. Gruber

A   E7   D

Verse 1

A
Silent night, holy night!

E7   **A**
All is calm, all is bright.

D   **A**
Round yon virgin Mother and Child.

D   **A**
Holy Infant, so tender and mild,

E7   **A**
Sleep in heavenly peace.

A   **E7**   **A**
Sleep in heavenly peace.

Verse 2

A
Silent night, holy night!

E7   **A**
Shepherds quake at the sight.

D   **A**
Glories stream from heaven afar.

D   **A**
Heav'nly hosts sing Alleluia,

E7   **A**
Christ, the Savior, is born.

A   **E7**   **A**
Christ, the Savior, is born.

Verse 3

A | |
Silent night, holy night!

E7 |A |
Son of God, love's pure light.

D |A |
Radiant beams from Thy holy face,

D |A |
With the dawn of re-deeming grace,

E7 |A |
Jesus, Lord at Thy birth.

A   E7 |A ||
Jesus, Lord at Thy birth.

So You Want to Be a Rock and Roll Star

Words and Music by
Roger McGuinn and Chris Hillman

G   A   D   E

132   21   123   2341

Verse 1

|G   A |G   A|
So you want to be a rock and roll star.
|G   A |G   A |
Then listen now to what I say.
|G   A |G   A|
Just get an elec - tric gui - tar
|G   A |G   A |
And take some time and learn how to play.
|D |E|
And with your hair swung right
|A |D ||
And your pants too tight, it's gonna be all right.

Verse 2

|G   A |G   A|
Then it's time to go   down - town,
|G   A |G   A |
Where the agent man won't let you down.
|G   A |G   A|
Sell your soul to the compa - ny
|G   A |G   A |
Who are waiting there to sell plastic-ware.
|D |E|
And in a week or two
|A |D ||
If you make the charts, the girls'll tear you apart.

Verse 3

```
       G          A            G        A
   The price you paid for your riches and fame,
      G        A            G   A              |
Was it all a strange   game? You're a little in - sane.
   G          A           G        A
   The money that came and the public ac - claim,
         G        A         G        A          |
Don't for - get what you are; you're a rock and roll   star.
   D        E
   La la la la la la
     A        D            ‖
La la la la la la la la la la.
```

Surfin' U.S.A.

Words and Music by Chuck Berry

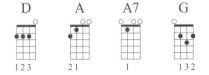

Verse 1

D **N.C.** |A |
If everybody had an ocean

A **N.C.** |D |
Across the U.S.A.,

D **N.C.** |A7 |
Then everybody'd be surfin'

A7 **N.C.** |D |
Like Californ - I - A.

D **N.C.** |G |
You'd see them wearing their bag - gies,

G **N.C.** |D |
Huarachi sandals too.

D **N.C.** |A |
A bushy, bushy blonde hairdo,

G **N.C.** |D |
Surfin' U.S.A.

Verse 2

```
D                           ‖A        |
    You'll catch 'em surfin' at Del Mar,
A                  |D        |
    Ventura County line,
D                |A7       |
    Santa Cruz and Trestles,
A7                    |D        |
    Australia's Narrabeen.
D           |G        |
    All over Man - hattan
G                       |D         |
    And down Doheny way.
D                |A       |
    Everybody's gone surfin',
G  N.C.        |D        |
    Surfin' U.S.A.
```

Verse 3

```
D  N.C.                      ‖A      |
    We'll all be planning out a route
A  N.C.                       |D       |
    We're gonna take real soon.
D  N.C.                   |A7        |
    We're waxing down our surfboards;
A7 N.C.              |D        |
    We can't wait for June.
D  N.C.                       |G       |
    We'll all be gone for the sum - mer;
G  N.C.              |D       |
    We're on safari to stay.
D  N.C.                  |A      |
    Tell the teacher we're surfin',
G  N.C.        |D        |
    Surfin' U.S.A.
```

Verse 4

```
       D                ‖A        |
         At Haggerty's and Swami's,
       A              |D        |
         Pacific Palisades,
       D                 |A7       |
         San Onofre and Sunset,
       A7                    |D        |
         Redondo Beach, L.A.
       D           |G       |
         All over La Jolla,
       G              |D         |
         At Waimea Bay.
       D                  |A      |
         Everybody's gone surfin',
       G  N.C.       |D       |        ‖
           Surfin' U.S.A.
```

Interlude

```
       A         |         |D        |        |        A        |        |         |
       D         |         |G        |        |D        |        |
```

Outro

```
       D                    ‖A       |
       Everybody's gone surfin',
    G  N.C.          |D       |
       Surfin' U.S.A.
    D  N.C.              |A       |
       Everybody's gone surfin',
    G  N.C.          |D       |
       Surfin' U.S.A.
    D  N.C.              |A       |
       Everybody's gone surfin',
    G  N.C.          |D       |
       Surfin' U.S.A.
    D     N.C.            |A       |
       Yeah, everybody's gone surfin',
    G  N.C.          |D       |
       Surfin' U.S.A.
    D     N.C.              |A       |
       Yeah, everybody's gone surfin',
    G  N.C.          |D       |       ‖
       Surfin' U.S.A.
```

Teach Your Children

Words and Music by Graham Nash

D G A Bm

Verse 1

D |G
You who are on the road

      |D |A
Must have a code that you can live by.

  |D |G
And so become your - self,

     |D |A ||
Because the past is just a goodbye.

Chorus 1

D |G
Teach your children well,

     |D |A
Their father's hell did slowly go by.

  |D |G
And feed them on your dreams,

     |D |A |
The one they pick's the one you'll know by.

D |G
  Don't you ever ask them why,

     |D
If they told you, you would cry,

      |Bm |G   A
So just look at them and sigh

    |D |G   D |A
And know they love you.

Verse 2

   ‖**D** |**G**
And you, of the tender years

            |**D** |**A**
Can't know the fears that your elders grew by.

        |**D** |**G**
And so please help them with your youth,

        |**D** |**A**   ‖
They seek the truth before they can die.

Chorus 2

D |**G**
Teach your parents well,

         |**D** |**A**
Their children's hell did slowly go by.

    |**D** |**G**
And feed them on your dreams,

           |**D** |**A** |
The one they pick's the one you'll know by.

D |**G**
  Don't you ever ask them why,

                     |**D**
If they told you, you would cry,

                |**Bm** |**G**   **A**
So just look at them and sigh

           |**D** |**G** |**D**   **A** |**D**   ‖
And know they love you.

This Land Is Your Land

Words and Music by Woody Guthrie

F   C   G7

Chorus

‖F |C |
This land is your land and this land is my land,

|G7 |C |
From Cali - fornia to the New York Island,

|F |C | |
From the redwood forest to the Gulf Stream waters,

G7 | |C |
This land was made for you and me.

Verse 1

‖F |C |
As I was walking that ribbon of highway,

|G7 |C |
I saw a - bove me that endless skyway.

|F |C | |
I saw be - low me that golden valley,

G7 | |C |
This land was made for you and me.

Repeat Chorus

Verse 2

     ‖**F** | |**C** |
I've roamed and rambled and I followed my footsteps

    |**G7** | |**C** |
To the sparkling sands of her diamond deserts.

   |**F** | |**C** | |
All a - round me, a voice was sounding,

G7 | |**C** |
"This land was made for you and me."

Repeat Chorus

Verse 3

     ‖**F** | |**C** |
When the sun came shining and I was strolling,

    |**G7** | |**C** |
And the wheat fields waving and the dust clouds rolling,

   |**F** | |**C** | |
As the fog was lifting a voice was chanting,

G7 | |**C** |
"This land was made for you and me."

Repeat Chorus

Verse 4

‖**F** | |**C** |
In the shadow of the steeple I saw my people,

|**G7** | |**C** |
By the relief office I seen my people.

|**F** | |**C** | |
As they stood there hungry, I stood there asking,

G7 | |**C** |
"Is this land made for you and me?"

Repeat Chorus

Verse 5

‖**F** | |**C** | |
Nobody living can ever stop me

|**G7** | |**C** |
As I go walking down that freedom highway,

|**F** | |**C** | |
Nobody living can ever make me turn back.

G7 | |**C** | ‖
This land was made for you and me.

Three Little Birds

Words and Music by
Bob Marley

A   D   E

21   234   2341

Intro

| A | | | |

Chorus

|| A |

Don't worry about a thing,

| D | A

'Cause every little thing gonna be all right.

| A |

Singin', "Don't worry about a thing,

| D | A

'Cause every little thing gonna be all right."

Verse

|| A | E

Rise up this morning, smiled with the rising sun.

| A | D

Three little birds   pitch by my doorstep,

| A | E

Singin' sweet songs of melodies pure and true,

| D   A |

Sayin', "This is my message to you-ou-ou." Singin',

Repeat Chorus

Repeat Verse

Repeat Chorus (2x)

Tom Dooley

Traditional Folksong

Verse 1

D
Hang your head, Tom Dooley,

D |**A**
Hang your head and cry.

A
Killed poor Laura Fos - ter.

|**A** |**D**
You know you bound to die.

Verse 2

||**D**
You took her on the hillside,

|**D** |**A**
As God Almighty knows.

|**A**
You took her on the hillside,

|**A** |**D**
And there you hid her clothes.

Verse 3

‖**D** |
You took her on the roadside,

|**D** |**A** |
Where you begged to be ex - cused.

|**A** |
You took her by the roadside,

|**A** |**D**
Where there you hid her shoes.

Verse 4

‖**D** |
You took her on the hillside

|**D** |**A** |
To make her be your wife.

|**A** |**A**
You took her on the hillside,

|**A** |**D** ‖
Where there you took her life.

Twist and Shout

Words and Music by
Bert Russell and Phil Medley

D   G   A7   A

Chorus

|D   G |A7
Well, shake it up, ba - by, now, (Shake it up, ba - by.)

|D   G |A7
Twist and shout. (Twist and shout.)

|D   G |A7
Come on, come on, come on, come on, baby, now, (Come on, ba - by.)

|D G |A7
Come on and work it on out. (Work it on out.)

Verse 1

||D G |A7
Well, work it on out. (Work it on out.)

|D   G |A7
You know you look so good. (Look so good.)

|D   G |A7
You know you got me goin', now, (Got me goin'.)

|D   G |A7
Just like I knew you would. (Like I knew you would,   oo.)

Repeat Chorus

Verse 2   ‖**D G** |**A7**
You know you twist, little girl,   (Twist little girl.)

              |**D**   **G** |**A7**
You know you twist so fine. (Twist so fine.)

                        |**D**   **G** |**A7**
Come on and twist a little closer, now, (Twist a little closer.)

                           |**D**   **G** |**A7**   ‖
And let me know that you're mine. (Let me know you're mine,   oo.)

Interlude   **A** | | |**A7** | |
              Ah, ah, ah, ah, wow!

Repeat Chorus

Repeat Verse 2

Outro   ‖**D**   **G** |**A7**
            Well, shake it, shake it, shake it, baby, now. (Shake it up, ba - by.)

             |**D**   **G** |**A7**
            Well, shake it, shake it, shake it, baby, now. (Shake it up, ba - by.)

             |**D**   **G** |**A7** |
            Well, shake it, shake it, shake it, baby, now. (Shake it up, ba - by.)

            A | | |**A7** |**D**   ‖
            Ah, ah, ah, ah.

Up on the Housetop

Words and Music by B.R. Handy

G   C   D7   G7

132   4   1113   213

Verse 1

G
Up on the housetop reindeer pause,

C   **G**   **D7**
Out jumps good old Santa Claus.

G
Down through the chimney with lots of toys,

C   **G**   **D7**   **G**
All for the little ones, Christmas joys.

Chorus

C   **G**
Ho, ho, ho, who wouldn't go?

D7   **G**
Ho, ho, ho, who wouldn't go?

G   **G7** **C**
Up on the house-top, click, click, click.

G   **D7**   **G**
Down through the chimney with good Saint Nick.

Verse 2

```
G                               |           |
First comes the stocking of little Nell,

C        G     |D7              |
Oh,  dear  Santa,  fill  it  well.

G                         |                   |
Give  her  a  dollie  that  laughs  and  cries,

C              G         |D7        G       ||
One  that  will  open  and  shut  her  eyes.
```

Repeat Chorus

Verse 3

```
G                               |           |
Next  comes  the  stocking  of  little  Will,

C        G         |D7              |
Oh,  just  see  what  a  glorious  fill!

G                         |           |
Here  is  a  hammer  and  lots  of  tacks,

C      G         |D7        G       ||
Also  a  ball  and  a  whip  that  cracks.
```

Repeat Chorus

Will the Circle Be Unbroken

Words by Ada R. Habershon
Music by Charles H. Gabriel

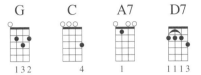

Verse 1

|G |
I was standing by my window

|C |G
On one cold and cloudy day,

|G |
When I saw the hearse come rollin'

|A7 |D7
For to take my mother a - way.

Chorus

‖G |
Will the circle be un - broken

|C |G
By and by Lord, by and by?

|C |G
There's a better home a - waiting

|D7 |G |
In the sky, in the sky.

Verse 2

‖**G** |
Oh, I told the under - taker,

|**C** |**G**
"Under - taker, please drive slow,

|**G** |
For this body you are hauling,

|**A7** |**D7**
Lord, I hate to see her go."

Repeat Chorus

Verse 3

‖**G** |
I will follow close be - hind her,

|**C** |**G**
Try to hold up and be brave,

|**G** |
But I could not hide my sorrow

|**A7** |**D7** ‖
When they laid her in the grave.

Repeat Chorus

Wild Montana Skies

Words and Music by
John Denver

D   G   A

Verse 1

|D |G |D |
He was born in the Bitterroot Valley in the early mornin' rain,

D | | |A
Wild geese over the wa-ter headin' north and home again,

|D | |G |D
Bringin' a warm wind from the south, bringin' the first taste of the spring,

|D | |A |D |
His mother took him to her breast and softly she did sing:

Chorus 1

||G |A |D |
Oh, oh, Mon-tana, give this child a home,

|G |A |D |
Give him the love of a good family and a woman of his own,

|G |A |D |G
Give him a fire in his heart, give him a light in his eyes,

|D | |A | |D | |G A D
Give him the wild wind for a broth-er and the wild Montana skies.

Verse 2

||D | |G |D
His mother died that summer, he never learned to cry.

|D | | |A
He never knew his fa-ther, he never did ask why.

|D | |G |D
And he never knew the an-swers that would make an easy way,

|D | |A |D |
But he learned to know the wil-derness and to be a man that way.

Verse 3

  ‖**D** | |**G** |**D**
His mother's brother took him in to his family and his home,

            |**D** | | |**A**
Gave him a hand   that he could lean on and a strength to call his own,

  |**D** | |**G** |**D**
And he learned to be a farm-er and he learned to love the land,

  |**D** | |**A** |**D** |
And he learned to read the sea-sons and he learned to make a stand.

Repeat Chorus 1

Verse 4

  ‖**D** | |**G** |**D**
On the eve of his twenty-first birthday he set out on his own.

  |**D** | | |**A**
He was thirty years and runnin' when he found his way back home,

    |**D** | |**G** |**D**
Ridin' a storm   across the moun-tains and an ach - in' in his heart,

  |**D** | |**A** |**D** |
Said he came to turn the pag-es and to make a brand-new start.

Verse 5

  ‖**D** | |**G** |**D**
Now he never told the story of the time that he was gone,

  |**D** | | |**A**
Some say he was a law-yer, some say he was a john.

  |**D** | |**G** |**D**
There was somethin' in the cit-y that he said he couldn't breathe,

    |**D** | |**A** |**D** |
And there was somethin' in the coun-try that he said he couldn't leave.

Repeat Chorus 1

Verse 6

    ‖D | |G |D

Now some say he was crazy, some are glad he's gone,

    |D | | |A

But some of us will miss him and we'll try to carry on,

    |D | |G |D

Giving a voice to the for-est, giving a voice to the dawn,

    |D | |A |D |

Giving a voice to the wil-derness and the land that he lived on.

Chorus 2

    ‖G |A |D |

Oh, oh, Mon-tana, give this child a home,

    |G |A |D |

Give him the love of a good family and a woman of his own,

    |G |A |D |G

Give him a fire in his heart, give him a light in his eyes,

    |D | |A | |D |

Give him the wild wind for a broth-er and the wild Montana skies.

Outro-Chorus

    ‖G |A |D |

Oh, oh, Mon-tana, give this child a home,

    |G |A |D |

Give him the love of a good family and a woman of his own,

    |G |A |D |G

Give him a fire in his heart, give him a light in his eyes,

    |D | |

Give him the wild wind for a broth-er and the

A | | | |D | |G A |D ‖

Wild   Montana skies.